Interfacing to Microprocessors

INTERFACING TO MICROPROCESSORS

J. C. Cluley

Senior Lecturer in Electronic and Electrical Engineering,
University of Birmingham, England

McGraw-Hill Book Company
New York St. Louis San Francisco Auckland
Bogotá Hamburg Johannesburg London Madrid
Mexico Montreal New Delhi Panama Paris
São Paulo Singapore Sydney Tokyo Toronto

First published in Great Britain by
The Macmillan Press Ltd.

Published in the U.S.A. by
McGraw-Hill Inc.

Printed in Hong Kong

ISBN 0–07–011409–9

Contents

Preface

The majority of the microprocessors now produced are installed as the controlling element in larger, generally non-electronic systems. Examples of these applications are domestic products such as cookers and washing machines, cash registers, weighing machines and much industrial process control and test equipment. The user is usually not aware that a microprocessor is embedded in the equipment, since it begins operations automatically when power is applied.

Although the microprocessor itself is produced in large quantities to a standard design, the extremely wide range of applications is reflected in the many different ways in which it must be interfaced to the outside world.

The design of these external circuits and their interactions with the microprocessor are the main topics of this book. Although the principles of data input and output with microprocessors are similar to those used with minicomputers, the detailed arrangements differ substantially. In particular, in order to afford the maximum flexibility in use, nearly all microprocessor input and output packages are programmable.

In planning the book I have assumed that the reader has some understanding of the way in which a microprocessor operates and how instructions are retrieved from the program store and executed. This information is well presented in *Understanding Microprocessors* by B. S. Walker (published by the Macmillan Press, London and John Wiley, New York) and I have not attempted to duplicate it. Although the book is mainly concerned with hardware and system design, I have included short program segments to illustrate the way in which interfaces can be controlled.

In chapter 4 I have included a brief survey of transducers. These are not always mentioned in many courses as they are not regarded as electronic devices. They are however essential features of many systems, and the availability of cheap and reliable transducers is often the critical factor in deciding whether a particular microprocessor application is economically justified.

I have given examples of the use of several of the more popular microprocessors, rather than confining the book to only one model, so as to give some indication of the variety of features and design philosophy available. Readers who require more information on the components in any particular family of microprocessors will need to consult the manufacturers' design data.

With the use of microprocessors now extending to a wide range of products, processes and equipment, there is a corresponding need for engineers and scientists in many disciplines to acquire an understanding of microprocessor applications and interfacing. This material is also being incorporated into many courses at universities and polytechnics.

I hope that this book will provide a satisfactory and comprehensive introduction to this developing and important subject.

J. C. CLULEY

1   Basic Microprocessor Architecture

1.1   Introduction

A microprocessor has been defined as 'an integrated circuit which performs the central processing function in a digital computer system'. The essential requirement for successful manufacture is a high volume of production, so that the very large cost of design and mask-making can be spread over typically hundreds of thousands of devices.

The problem of the microprocessor user is to take this standard product and tailor it to the particular requirements of his own environment and application. The main aspects of this operation are the unique program of instructions which determines the action of the microprocessor, and the way in which it is attached or 'interfaced' to the system with which it operates.

In this book we are concerned mainly with the design and arrangement of the interface, and to a lesser extent with programming. The program examples given show how data transfers can be effected, how the state of external devices can be tested and how they can be controlled. Program design and strategy will not be discussed in any detail.

1.2   Components of a Microprocessor System

A microprocessor alone is unable to perform any useful actions. In order to work successfully it must be connected to other units, generally on a shared or 'party line' basis, so as to provide all the functions of a complete computing system. A typical arrangement is shown in figure 1.1, and comprises in addition to the microprocessor the following items.

(a)   Program store

This is a read-only device, which has been programmed during manufacture (masked ROM), or by the user (fusible link PROM or erasable PROM). It is supplied with an address, control and timing signals, and will then drive on to the data lines the contents of the location addressed.

(b)   Data store

This is writable storage (usually referred to as RAM) used for holding information upon which the computer is operating. It has the same set of connections

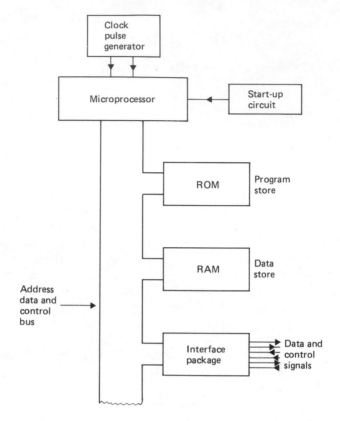

Figure 1.1 The components of a basic microprocessor system

as the program store but in addition needs control signals to order either a read or a write operation.

(c) Peripheral interface packages

Some external devices can be connected directly to the microprocessor, but for an output operation data storage is almost invariably required. In addition, various status flags and timing signals may be required, and it is thus usually much simpler to use the manufacturer's input/output (I/O) interface package than to construct an interface using a number of small-scale integrated circuits. Most applications require parallel data transfers but serial data are needed for feeding data over telephone lines or attaching VDUs and teleprinters. Interface packages are available which incorporate all of the necessary logic for these applications within a single package.

(d) Clock pulse supply

Microprocessors require a continuous train of pulses to synchronise internal and external events, or for some versions two non-overlapping pulse trains. These clock pulses were originally generated by a separate package, their frequency being determined by a quartz resonator.

Later microprocessors included the clock pulse generator circuits, so that the only external component required was the quartz crystal.

(e) Start-up circuit

In order that the microprocessor shall set its internal registers in the proper state when the power is first applied, it is necessary to earth the reset or restart pin for some milliseconds before returning it to its normal +5 V level. This action may be performed either by a trigger circuit which senses the 5 V supply, or by a simple C–R circuit, both external to the microprocessor package.

1.3 Bus Lines and Bus Signals

The connections which link together the processor, the program and data stores and the peripheral units are called a 'bus' and can conveniently be separated into three groups, the data bus, the address bus and the control and timing bus. The bus lines cannot use conventional logic packages because they are required in some cases to operate in different directions at different times.

Thus for a 'write' operation data must flow along the data bus from a processor register to a peripheral device or to the data store. In a 'read' operation the direction of the data flow is reversed, and information from external sources is read into a processor register. In order to allow this bidirectional operation, devices which drive the bus are usually designed to have three output states, logic 1 output (high), logic 0 output (low) and off. In the off condition the circuit presents a high impedance to the bus, so allowing its potential to be determined by some other device connected to the bus. This arrangement is called 'tri-state' drive and is usually provided by two series transistors as shown in figure 1.2(a).

An alternative arrangement sometimes used on lightly loaded lines is the 'open-drain' circuit of figure 1.2(b). Here the single transistor is cut off when the device is not transmitting data, and is only turned on when transmitting a logical 0. A single resistor in the range 2–10 kΩ is connected between the bus line and +5 V to hold the bus at logic 1 level when no driver is energised. This circuit has the disadvantage that its positive-going transition is rather slow, being determined by the product of the resistor value and the total stray capacitance of the bus. The tri-state circuit has a much faster transition since the upper transistor is fully conducting to signal a logic 1 and its resistance is typi-

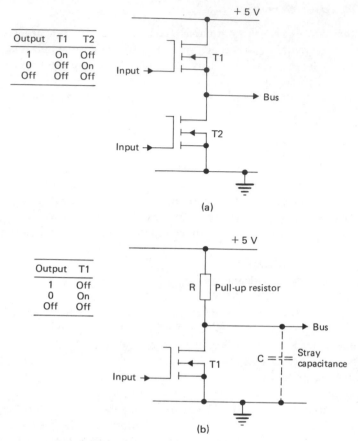

Output	T1	T2
1	On	Off
0	Off	On
Off	Off	Off

+ 5 V

Input →

T1

Bus

Input →

T2

(a)

Output	T1
1	Off
0	On
Off	Off

+ 5 V

R Pull-up resistor

Bus

$C =$ Stray capacitance

Input →

T1

(b)

Figure 1.2 (a) Tri-state bus driver; (b) open-drain bus driver

cally only a few hundred ohms. Consequently all bus lines which are liable to substantial capacitance loading and require bidirectional working (the data and address buses particularly) are normally driven by tri-state circuits.

Unlike fast minicomputers, the bus lines are usually confined to one or two printed circuit boards, are relatively quite short, and so do not need to be treated as transmission lines or be properly terminated. This saves a great deal of power and allows transistors with much lower current ratings to be used.

To indicate typical values, we note that the specification of the M6800 microprocessor puts an upper limit of 130 pF on the total capacitance loading of the data bus lines.

Assuming a system with this capacitance and a pull-up resistor of 3.3 kΩ the time constant for a positive-going transition with the open-drain driver circuit of figure 1.2(b) is given by

$$T = CR$$
$$= 130 \times 10^{-12} \times 3300 \text{ s}$$
$$= 0.43 \ \mu s$$

The 10–90 per cent rise time is then

$$T_R = 2.2 \ T$$
$$= 0.95 \ \mu s$$

Clearly this is much too long if the microprocessor has a 1 MHz clock rate and must thus handle pulses which are typically 0.5 μs long. The arrangement however is generally used for control lines which are active only on the negative-going transition and have no critical timing on the positive-going (slower) transition. Typical of these is an interrupt request line which is connected only to peripheral devices, not to storage packages, and so has less loading than the data lines.

Note that in this case the important negative-going transition will be much faster, because the resistive component of the time constant is almost entirely the drain-source resistance of the driver transistor, which will be considerably less than 3.3 kΩ.

If the calculation above is repeated for the tri-state circuit, using a typical driver resistance value of 300 Ω, the time constant is eleven times less and the rise and fall times are both 86 ns. This neglects any switching time for the transistor; if some allowance is included for this, the rise and fall times would be in the region of 100 ns.

Taking this value, the mean transistor current during the rise or fall of bus voltage is given by

$$i = \frac{CV}{t} = \frac{100 \times 10^{-12} \times 5}{100 \times 10^{-9}} \quad \text{A}$$

$$= 5 \text{ mA}$$

For a 1 MHz pulse rate each transistor will conduct for only 100 ns in each 1 μs, so giving an average current of only 0.5 mA. These peak and mean currents are well within the capacity of the physically small transistor of the microprocessor and its supporting packages. If however the bus lines are so long that they need correct terminations at both ends, as in some minicomputers, the driver current needed to pull the bus voltage down to 0 V may exceed 50 mA.

Microprocessor systems with a number of store packages and peripheral devices attached to the lines may give a total bus capacitance which exceeds the permitted figure. In this case the bus must be split into sections using buffers or bus-extenders, so that no section has more than the permitted loading.

The type of device used depends upon the nature of the bus line. For unidirectional lines such as the clock and interrupt lines and the address lines, a simple unity-gain amplifier suffices, but for the data lines which have to transfer information in both directions two amplifiers connected back-to-back as shown in figure 1.3 are used. In order to prevent oscillation or latch-up, the amplifiers are switched or gated, and arranged so that only one is operative at a time. The control line is connected to the read/write bus, so that the outgoing (from the microprocessor) amplifier operates for write, and the incoming amplifier for read.

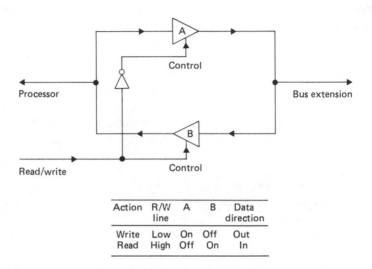

Action	R/W line	A	B	Data direction
Write	Low	On	Off	Out
Read	High	Off	On	In

Figure 1.3 Bidirectional bus driver

1.4   Signal Flow During Data Transfers

We first consider the action needed during the output or write instruction which transmits a byte of data in parallel over the data lines. Since this will be present on the bus for usually less than a microsecond, some form of storage is necessary, as few if any devices can operate correctly with such a brief sample of data. The interface needs to perform the following functions

(a) Detect that the processor is making a data transfer involving this particular interface. This normally requires the recognition of either an address or a device number on the address lines.

(b) Detect that the processor is executing a write transfer. This involves sensing either the read/write line or the write strobe line.

(c) Detect the correct moment when the data are present on the data bus and available for storage. This involves sensing either a clock pulse or the write strobe pulse.

Generally the three signals resulting from (a), (b) and (c) are ANDed together to provide a clock pulse for a set of D-type bistables. The D terminals are permanently connected to the data lines, so that after the clock pulse the data transferred will be stored and available at the Q output of the bistable. It will remain until the next data transfer occurs.

To ensure that the output is in a known state when the power is first applied, the clear terminals of the bistables may be connected to the reset or restart line so that when power is applied to the system the device register is automatically cleared.

Before a data transfer occurs it may be necessary to examine a status flag in the interface to ensure that the device is ready to accept data. Usually a complete byte will be read from a control and status register, and one bit of this will be examined.

For a read operation no storage is generally provided. The functions required are

(a) As for a write operation (address sensing).

(b) Detect that the processor is executing a read instruction, using the read/write line or the read strobe.

(c) Detect when the processor requires the data to be gated on to the data lines. This timing information is derived from a clock pulse or a read strobe.

Again the three signals from (a), (b) and (c) are ANDed together, this time to provide a gating signal which turns on a tri-state driver which puts the data on to the data lines.

Other signals may need gating into the combined load signal, depending upon the processor, for example valid memory address (VMA) or input/output request (IORQ).

These input and output logic circuits can be assembled from small-scale integrated circuits but it is generally simpler to use the manufacturer's parallel I/O package which includes storage for output transfers and data bus drivers, in addition to control registers. These will be described in more detail in chapter 3 where the characteristics of some current I/O packages are discussed.

1.5 Input/Output Transfer Methods

Having considered the principles governing the logic of input and output operations, we next examine the program instructions involved, and the processor actions which take place. We can distinguish three different arrangements, generally called program-controlled transfers, interrupt driven transfers and direct memory access (DMA) or autonomous transfer.

Program-controlled transfers are the simplest from both the hardware and software aspects. They occur when the program executes an I/O instruction, consequently the instant of transfer is decided by the program alone. Since this is not synchronised with the activities of the peripheral device there may be a conflict if the processor, for example, outputs data when the device is not ready to accept them. The data would then be lost.

In order to prevent this, a bistable or 'flag' is incorporated into the interface package, which can be set by the device and read by the processor. If we assume that the device sets the flag to logic 1 when it is ready for data, the program is arranged to test the flag, and if it is not set, to continue testing it. When the device sets the flag the program will branch to an output instruction which transfers the data. For convenience the data transfer is usually arranged to clear the flag ready for the next transaction. The loop of instructions which precedes the transfer is generally called a 'waiting loop' and the sequence is of the form

> READ CONTROL REGISTER

TEST FLAG BIT

BRANCH BACK IF NOT SET

OUTPUT DATA TO DEVICE

This is sometimes called 'wait and go' operation, and it allows the program execution to be delayed until the device is ready. However, it will not allow program execution to be accelerated if the device is ready before the I/O transfer instruction is reached.

Difficulties may arise if several devices are attached to the processor, since a device which is not ready will hold up the program and prevent any other device from being serviced.

An alternative program strategy to that given above is to test each device and, if it is not ready, branch to test the next device. Each device is tested in turn and only when a device is found which is ready for data transfer does the program branch to effect the transfer. The procedure is called 'polling' and requires the processor to remain in a loop; this may include some other processor action if time permits. The essential requirement is that even in the worst case, when every device is serviced, each one is polled often enough to input or output all the data required, without missing any. Generally the maximum data rate for each device is known, and the critical time is the time between data transfers required by the fastest device. The longest time to execute a loop of the program must be somewhat less than this. For example the maximum data rate for a teleprinter is ten characters per second. Thus any processor which has a teleprinter attached to a parallel data port must poll the port at intervals of less than one-tenth of a second to determine whether a character has been received by the port.

The basic structure of the polling routine is

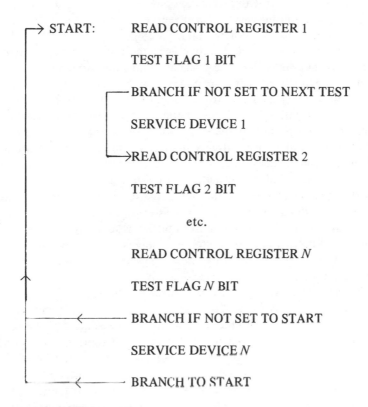

START: READ CONTROL REGISTER 1

TEST FLAG 1 BIT

BRANCH IF NOT SET TO NEXT TEST

SERVICE DEVICE 1

READ CONTROL REGISTER 2

TEST FLAG 2 BIT

etc.

READ CONTROL REGISTER N

TEST FLAG N BIT

BRANCH IF NOT SET TO START

SERVICE DEVICE N

BRANCH TO START

The instruction 'SERVICE DEVICE I' is usually a JUMP TO SUBROUTINE instruction, so that the program after completing the subroutine will return to test the flag connection to the device next on the list.

1.6   Interrupts

Although polling is a satisfactory process for a set of attached devices with roughly similar data rates, it cannot be used with fast devices if many other interfaces are also active. In such a case the fast devices need rapid service and there is no time to test all the other devices first. The solution is to use a program interrupt.

This means that the device requiring attention can cause the processor to leave the program that it is currently executing, and transfer to the device service routine. At the end of the routine the processor must resume its execution of the previous program.

The action is broadly similar to that which occurs when the processor executes a subroutine, but with two exceptions

(a) The service routine may be involved at any time, and so at any stage during the execution of the main program.

(b) The branch of the service routine is caused not by an instruction in the main program, but by an electrical signal originating from the device itself.

Although the interrupt signal may occur at any time, in order to avoid errors and misdirected data the processor must take action only when it has completed the execution of one instruction and before it fetches the next.

Usually the control unit of the processor is designed to pass through a set of states between ending one instruction and fetching the next, so that it tests each of the interrupt request lines in turn, branching into the interrupt handling sequence as soon as it finds one which is active and enabled.

A further requirement for dealing with interrupts is that, regardless of the point reached in the main program, all registers in the processor must contain exactly the same data after returning from the interrupt as they did immediately before the interrupt. Thus the contents of any registers used by the service routine must be saved before using them, and restored immediately before returning to the main program.

Finally the processor must return control to the instruction immediately following that which was executed just before the interrupt occurred. This requires the processor to store the 'return link' or the address of the following instruction before embarking on the interrupt service routine. This is obtained directly from the program counter which will contain the address of the first byte of the following instruction. Usually this is done automatically by the processor which puts the return link on to the stack. Some microprocessors also store the contents of their registers on the stack, but generally instructions are required in the service program for this.

As an example let us assume that the stack pointer register contains address A078 (hexadecimal) and that an interrupt occurs during the execution of an instruction in locations 0100 and 0101. If the interrupt facility is enabled, the interrupt line will be tested at the end of each instruction execution, before fetching the next instruction. At this stage the program counter will have been incremented to point to the first byte of the next instruction, in location 0102. This is the return link and it will be transferred to the empty location A078 at the top of the stack, and its adjacent location A077 (being a 16-bit address it requires 2 bytes). During this time the stack pointer will have been decremented twice and will now contain A076. The contents of further processor registers may now be put on to the stack, before starting any data handling within the service routine. At the end of the routine the processor registers will be reloaded from the stack, and the instruction 'Return from Interrupt' will pull the return link from the stack, transfer it to the program counter and the processor will enter the 'Fetch' state. It will fetch the next instruction in the main program and continue its execution.

The interrupt action may be controlled either globally or individually. Most microprocessor interrupt lines are 'maskable', that is, they can be enabled or disabled by a program instruction. Also the control register in each port of the interface package can usually be programmed to control whether setting the device flag also creates an interrupt. For convenience it is usual for the interrupt to be disabled when the processor is first switched on, also as soon as an interrupt has been accepted.

A point so far ignored is the choice of address to which the processor branches to begin the service routine. This depends on the particular processor, the simplest option being a fixed address as used on the Motorola M6800. This gives rapid action if only one device is attached to the interrupt line but, if more than one device can create an interrupt, the first action in the service routine must be a poll of all interrupt flags, in order to determine which device is requesting service.

A faster option is available for up to eight devices in the Intel 8080; the device requesting service puts a 3-bit address on to the data lines, so selecting one of eight possible starting addresses for the service routine. The Z80 microprocessor has much greater flexibility; it generates a 16-bit address taking one byte from the device and a second byte from a special interrupt register in the processor. It can also use the simpler scheme described for the 8080.

This process of using hardware to generate the address of the service routine is called 'vectoring' and the number generated is called the 'vector address'.

1.7 Direct Memory Access

Even if interrupts use hardware vectoring, and so avoid having to execute a polling program, they require a number of instructions for each item of data handled. For the very simple case of reading a set of waveform samples and storing them in a block reserved in the store, the following actions must occur for each sample

(1) Read sample into accumulator.
(2) Copy into store.
(3) Increment address for next data item.
(4) Test whether enough readings have been taken to fill the space allocated in the store.

Also the 'housekeeping' activity of storing the return link, saving and restoring registers is needed.

All of this means that very fast data streams such as may come from another processor, or a wind tunnel experiment, for example, do not allow enough time between data for interrupt servicing.

One solution is the use of direct memory access or DMA. This avoids the bottleneck created by the processor, and allows the external device to communicate directly with the store. During this the processor is disabled, and the address, data and control signals are supplied by the device interface.

This process requires a short program to initialise various registers, in particular to supply the address of the first byte in the store which has been reserved for the data, and the number of bytes to be transferred. The final instruction allows the device to control the DMA interface; thereafter no program is needed and each byte which becomes available is arranged to generate a DMA request signal to the processor. This, as with interrupts, cannot act immediately and is usually designed to wait until the current store cycle has ended. It then emits a DMA grant instruction, and ceases operation, putting the drivers on the data, address and control buses into the high impedance state.

A counter in the DMA interface is usually decremented by each byte transferred, and when it reaches zero an interrupt is usually generated to deal with the block of data. Data and control signals are supplied by the device interface. Data can equally well be fed from the processor store out to the DMA interface by the same process. The data may either be sent across as a block, or a byte at a time (usually called 'cycle-stealing'), depending upon the data rate needed by the DMA channel.

Most manufacturers provide a special DMA package for this method of data transfer, which may include several different inputs for requesting DMA action. These are handled according to a specified priority order, each channel having a programmable register to hold the address of the next byte to be transferred, and the number of bytes awaiting transfer. Each DMA transfer increments the address register and decrements the byte counter, stopping when the latter reaches zero.

In this chapter we have examined in outline the basic architecture of typical 8-bit microprocessor systems and the various ways in which information can be exchanged with external devices. In the following chapter we consider input and output transfers in more detail, the way in which the processor selects a particular interface, and some of the instructions available for I/O transfers.

2 Principles of Data Transfer

2.1 Device Addressing

In order to transfer data reliably to and from external devices in a bus or 'party-line' structure such as a microprocessor system, it is essential to provide the processor with the facility to select one device register to communicate with. All other register and storage areas must remain in the off state to prevent mutilation of the data. The selection is arranged by allocating a unique address (usually 16 bits) or device code (usually 8 bits) to each register in the interface. Logic is provided at each interface which ensures that any device code can energise only the required register and will not select any other.

Systems which employ coding generally provide two byte input/output instructions, the first byte containing the operation code, and the second byte the device code. The form is

IN   10

or OUT 12

When executing for example the IN 10 instruction the register number 10 is placed on the lower 8 address lines, and a timing pulse informs the external device when to gate the data byte on to the data lines. To ensure that no program or data store can be accessed an IORQ (I/O request) pulse is sent out on one of the bus control lines. This is gated in with the address decoding logic, so that only when both the device code and the IORQ appear does the interface respond. The RAM and ROM storage is prevented from responding because these require, as well as an address, the MEMRQ (memory request) line to be energised. MEMRQ is only activated when the program needs access to either ROM or RAM; in this case IORQ is not energised.

Standard parallel I/O packages handle a byte of data at a time, and in order to communicate with each of the two ports which serve the outside world, and with their control registers, they require four separate device codes. These are generally arranged in sequence by connecting the two 'register select' pins on the package to the two least significant address lines A0 and A1. The 8 address lines then enable us to encode 256 different device codes, enough for 64 two-port packages.

Far fewer than this suffice for nearly all applications, and we can then simplify the device selection logic by examining only some of the 8 address lines. In this case more than one device code will select a particular device register.

This is of no consequence provided that the particular device code allocated to each register cannot activate any other register.

For example, in a system having only four I/O packages each package need only be connected to one address line in addition to A0 and A1 which select the four internal registers. One possible arrangement is shown in figure 2.1, which for clarity omits several control signals such as read/write (R/W), IORQ, and timing pulses. Each package has a 'chip select' pin CS which must be at logic 1 to activate it. Thus we can connect packages A–D to address lines A2–A5 for chip selection and to A0–A1 for register selection.

The codes which activate the packages are

Package	Binary codes	Hexadecimal codes
A	0000 01XX	04 – 07
B	0000 10XX	08 – 0B
C	0001 00XX	10 – 13
D	0010 00XX	20 – 23

The bits XX can have four values 00, 01, 10 and 11 to select one of the four registers in the package.

Since each package decoding logic tests only 3 out of the 8 address lines, leaving 5 as 'don't care' inputs, each device register will respond to $2^5 = 32$ different codes in all. However the codes given in the table will not activate any other device, and so may be used safely. Note that codes FC, 7C, or 3C would activate all four interfaces. If all four devices performed an output transfer, this would enable a 'broadcast' output to occur. Such a process however is hardly ever used, since we could not read four different control registers simultaneously to ensure that the devices were ready to accept data.

The procedure described above is called 'partial decoding' and it is used wherever possible to minimise the amount of logic needed. It does however complicate matters if we need subsequently to expand the system. For example the scheme shown in figure 2.1 could be extended to handle two further packages using address lines A6 and A7, but if we needed to attach any further packages it would be necessary to decode at least two address lines in addition to A0 and A1 in order to select any particular package.

As mentioned above, the diagram in figure 2.1 is simplified by omitting other control lines. Generally a CE (chip enable) pin would be used. This must be held at logic 1, during data transfer, otherwise the chip is isolated from the data lines. A convenient signal for the CE pin is the IORQ line. This is high only during I/O operations, and thus instructions which access program and data stores would not cause an IORQ pulse and so could not activate the peripheral device registers.

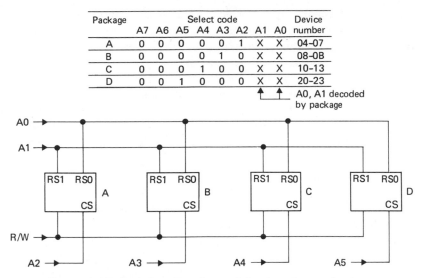

| Package | Select code | | | | | | | | Device |
	A7	A6	A5	A4	A3	A2	A1	A0	number
A	0	0	0	0	0	1	X	X	04–07
B	0	0	0	0	1	0	X	X	08–0B
C	0	0	0	1	0	0	X	X	10–13
D	0	0	1	0	0	0	X	X	20–23

A0, A1 decoded
by package

Figure 2.1 Partial decoding for peripheral package selection

2.2 Memory-mapped Input/Output

The above procedure for input and output is similar to that used on early minicomputers but has two major disadvantages. The first is the very limited set of operations which can be performed on the device registers. These can either be loaded from the processor or read by the processor. By comparison the contents of a store location can typically be the subject of a much greater range of operations such as

Clear

Increment

Decrement

Test (compare with zero)

Compare (with a specified value)

Add to accumulator

Subtract from accumulator

in addition to loading and reading.

The second limitation is in the register associated with loading and reading. This is normally the accumulator only, whereas the contents of a store location may be loaded from or read into several other processor registers.

These difficulties were surmounted in some minicomputers (notably the PDP-11 family) by treating the interface registers in exactly the same manner as storage locations, and allocating them addresses in the total address space available. This procedure is called 'memory-mapped I/O' in microprocessor systems and is a normal feature of some models, for example the 6800. It can however be used in other types such as the 8080 range which also have IN N and OUT N instructions.

The only complication which arises is that the addresses allocated for the device registers are in the same address space as that of the RAM and ROM packages, involving 16 address lines. Thus it is normally necessary to decode more address lines using memory-mapped I/O since we must distinguish not only each interface register from all other interface registers but also from all of the program, data and stack storage areas accessible to the processor.

As with the use of device select coding, the designers' aim is usually to allocate the various sections of storage within the total address space so as to minimise the amount of decoding logic required. Frequently the program and data storage areas are located in the top and bottom of the storage space, with the interface packages near the middle.

As an example the address space might be allocated as follows

Data storage	0000 – 0FFF
Interface registers	8000 – 80FF
Program storage	E000 – FFFF

using hexadecimal notation.

Here it is convenient to decode the two most significant address lines. These serve to distinguish between the three storage areas. Generally each package has several chip select inputs which must be energised to activate the package. These are used, often with additional logic, to select unambiguously a particular package.

In this case the two most significant address lines can be decoded to select which storage area is accessed, as follows

Storage area accessed	*A15*	*A14*
Data storage (RAM)	0	0
Interface	1	0
Program storage (ROM)	1	1

We could also allocate another block of storage starting at, say, address 4000 for PROM or a data stack, with the address code $A15 = 0$, $A14 = 1$.

A convenient method would be to use a 1-out-of-4 decoder, for example,

4028 (CMOS) or 74LS 138 (TTL), with the two inputs connected to A15 and A14, and the four outputs connected respectively to RAM, PROM, interfaces and ROM.

We assume that the system has four interface packages, A,B,C,D, each of which has a direct and a negated chip select line CS0 and $\overline{CS1}$, and that the addresses allocated are as shown in figure 2.2. Each package has its chip select line connected to a different address line in the group A2–A5, and the negated chip select input $\overline{CS1}$ is driven by a NAND gate connected to A15 and A14.

As before, each package has four adjacent addresses which serve to select the various internal registers by signals on A0 and A1.

Package	Address	Address lines			
		15 14 13 12	11 10 9 8	7 6 5 4	3 2 1 0
RAM	0000–0FFF	0 0 0 0	D D D D	D D D D	D D D D
ROM	E000–FFFF	1 1 1 D	D D D D	D D D D	D D D D
Interface A	8004–8007	1 0 0 0	0 0 0 0	0 0 0 0	0 1 D D
Interface B	8008–800B	1 0 0 0	0 0 0 0	0 0 0 0	1 0 D D
Interface C	8010–8013	1 0 0 0	0 0 0 0	0 0 0 1	0 0 D D
Interface D	8020–8023	1 0 0 0	0 0 0 0	0 0 1 0	0 0 D D

D indicates address lines decoded on chip

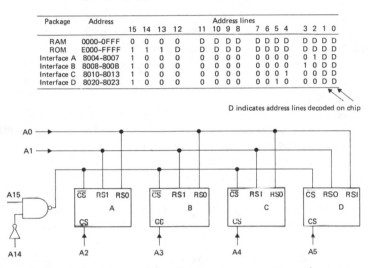

Figure 2.2 Partial decoding of memory-mapped input/output

In a complete circuit diagram each package would also require a clock pulse train for timing, a read/write signal, and perhaps also VMA. VMA (valid memory address) indicates that the information on the address lines is a memory address and not a 16-bit number being moved within the processor.

Some development systems which include storage allocations for an extra PROM, more user data storage, etc., may use a 1-out-of-8 decoder attached to A15, A14 and A13 to decode the top three address lines. This then allows us to specify eight separate storage areas and to select any one of them by using the appropriate address on A15, A14 and A13.

2.3   Input/Output Package Design

As in the design of the microprocessor itself, the manufacturer of an I/O package always tries to make it adaptable to the widest range of applications to enable the economic advantages of mass production to be realised. In order to cater for diverse uses, most packages are made programmable. Thus in addition to registers which handle data, they incorporate control registers which can be loaded before handling data in order to determine, for example

whether a status flag is set on the rising or falling edge of the input
whether the data lines connecting the package to the external device are outputs or inputs
whether an interrupt is created when the status flag is set
for serial transmission, how many data bits comprise a character,
etc.

The range of options which are available from a package depends upon its complexity, the ultimate being a package with a microprocessor, a small program store and some data store incorporated. This enables tasks such as code conversion and preliminary data processing to be effected without recourse to the central processor.

The function of the I/O package is to act as a data exchange point between the processor running at a fixed speed and the external device which is operating generally at a much lower rate, and perhaps quite irregularly.

A widely used package provides parallel I/O, generally via two 8-bit ports. In addition to a data register, each port has a control and status register, and in some cases a register controlling the direction in which the port handles data.

Usually some control lines are also provided to enable the processor to sense the state of the peripheral device, and to signal to it that the processor has sent a byte of data.

As shown in figures 2.1 and 2.2, two register select inputs allow the processor to select one of four internal registers to read or write. Manufacturers have somewhat divergent views about the optimum package design, and the particular features of several widely used I/O packages are described in the following chapter.

2.4 Combined Interface Packages

A standing complaint about all microprocessor families in the early days was the large number of packages needed to produce a useful system. In order to counter this some manufacturers in about the third generation of devices produced packages which combined parallel I/O interfaces and RAM or ROM. This, claimed the manufacturers, enabled the user to assemble a three-chip system, comprising

(1) processor, clock circuits and start-up circuit
(2) RAM for data store and interface registers
(3) ROM or PROM and interface registers

In some chip sets the RAM package contains a counter/timer in addition to external ports.

The final step on this path of development is the 'single-chip' microprocessor which several manufacturers now produce. This comprises an 8-bit microprocessor, clock and start-up circuits, 50—100 bytes of RAM and 1K or 2K bytes of ROM, together with two or three 8-bit ports. Some compromises are needed on account of the limit of 40 pins for external connections. The particular features of these devices are described in chapter 5.

2.5   Counter/Timer Packages

Many microprocessor applications involve counting external events, or generating fixed time delays by counting clock cycles or an external pulse train. Although the microprocessor can easily perform these tasks, it cannot easily perform other actions at the same time.

A major difficulty arises in a system which uses interrupts, since any events which occur during the execution of the interrupt service routine will not be recorded by the main program.

A convenient way of overcoming these problems and releasing the central processor for other tasks is to provide hardware which can perform the counting task without intervention from the processor, usually creating an interrupt when a fixed time delay or count is reached. Otherwise the computer can read the accumulated total count at any convenient time.

The hardware is usually built into a single counter/timer package, containing typically three 16-bit binary counters, three control registers and one or more status registers.

The packages are programmable, and can count either external events or, by counting pulses of a known frequency, generate fixed time intervals. Typically the counter can be loaded by the processor, then enabled, and external pulses will then decrement it down to zero. When this occurs a flag is set in the status register and an interrupt can be generated if necessary. Also if some external action is needed a pulse can be generated by the package.

For generating known time intervals, the pulses can be supplied either by the processor clock or by an external source of known frequency.

2.6   Serial Input/Output

Although byte-parallel input and output matches most nearly the data flow inside the microprocessor, the extension of eight data lines, a common return and the one or two control lines is much too expensive where the peripheral device is more than perhaps 100 feet from the I/O port.

For these remote data stations serial transmission, which requires only one send, one receive line and a common return, is much cheaper. In consequence a frequent requirement is a serial I/O package which converts a parallel byte of data into a serial pulse train for transmission, and serial to parallel for reception. In order to permit satisfactory reception the bit rate must be exactly controlled, usually by counting down a crystal oscillator.

For slow data rates, up to 600–1200 bauds (bits per second) the transmission is normally asynchronous in that each byte or character sent is not related in time to the preceding or following character. This requires some control bits to signal the start and end of the character. Usually a complete character is encoded in the following sequence

(1) 1 start bit
(2) 5–8 data bits
(3) parity bit if used
(4) 2 stop bits

As with parallel interfaces, these packages are programmable, having control and status registers in addition to data registers.

The programmable options are typically

(1) character length of 5,6,7 or 8 bits
(2) odd-parity, even-parity or no-parity bit
(3) division ratio of 1, 16 or 64 times between clock input and serial bit rate

The optional parity bit allows a simple test to be carried out at the receiver to detect whether one bit in the character has become corrupted.

For example, if both transmitting and receiving package have been programmed for odd parity, the additional parity bit will be added to the data character so that the total number of 1's is an odd number. If any single bit is corrupted during transmission the received signal will contain an even number of 1's. The receiving package will detect this and signal a parity error. It is of course impossible to detect a double error by this means, but if the error rate is not too large a double error is unlikely. For example if the chance of any one character being corrupted is 10^{-5}, the chance of one bit in a 9-bit block being in error is 9×10^{-5}. The chance of an undetected double error is

$$\frac{10^{-10} \times 9 \times 8}{2} \quad = \quad 3.6 \times 10^{-9}$$

At 300 bauds this is one error on average in about 250 hours of transmission. This is an oversimplified calculation which assumes that interference arises from voltage spikes shorter in duration than 1 bit.

The receiver also checks the number of data bits in each incoming character and, should this differ from the expected number programmed into the package, an error will be signalled.

The package usually caters for full duplex working, that is, independent send and receive channels operating simultaneously. In order to maintain the fastest data flow possible, the transmitting channel is designed to signal to the processor as soon as the transmitter buffer store is empty, so that a further byte can be sent to it.

Similarly, as soon as an entire character has been received, the package signals the processor to read it, so that it can be safely stored before the succeeding byte replaces it. The receiver automatically strips off the start and stop bits and the parity bit before sending the received byte in parallel on to the data bus.

The procedure described above is called asynchronous operation, since there is no fixed time interval between characters. The receiver detects the start of each character as a transition from mark to space, or logic 1 to logic 0. It then samples the input again after half a bit period, which should occur in the middle of the start bit. If the input is still space, the receiver accepts it as a genuine starting bit, and samples the remainder of the character in the middle of each bit period. Thus the receiving clock signal must keep in synchronism with the transmitting clock only for the fraction of a second needed for sending a complete character.

This protocol was developed for mechanical teleprinters which were governed in speed by centrifugal governors. Now by electronic techniques we can use a constant-frequency crystal oscillator to determine the transmitting clock frequency, and lock the receiving clock oscillator on to the received data train. This enables a continuous train of bits to be transmitted without starting or stop bits, so saving 3 bits in every 11.

Asynchronous operation is generally used at speeds of 1200 bauds and below, and synchronous operation at speeds above this. The main detection problem is then to decide where one character ends and the next starts. This is determined by initially sending several SYNC (synchronising) characters when the transmission begins. The receiving interface package switches to the search mode when power is initially applied, and examines each successive group of 8 adjacent bits for a match to the SYNC character which has been programmed into it. When this is detected the receiving package has detected a complete character, and it then takes each subsequent group of 8 bits as a character. The detection of a SYNC character enables the receiver to switch to its normal receiving mode, in which characters are staticised by a shift register and sent in parallel to the data bus.

Some manufacturers provide separate synchronous and asynchronous communications packages; others provide only one which can be set for either mode of operation.

Some packages have facilities for optionally searching for two successive SYNC characters, and only then switching to the normal receiving mode. The initial SYNC characters are not sent to the receiving processor.

Clearly this process needs a continuous stream of characters available from the sending processor or data source. If this is not available the sending interface will insert dummy SYNC characters to fill out the bit stream, and these will be deleted by the receiver.

In this chapter we have examined the general requirements for interfacing to a microprocessor and the features of serial and parallel I/O packages. In the following chapter we consider in more detail the characteristics of some particular packages which are widely used for interfacing.

3   Input/Output Packages

3.1   Parallel Input/Output Packages — the M6820 and M6821

Most parallel I/O packages provide two 8-bit external ports together with additional control and status lines. Typical of these is the Motorola M6821. This was originally produced as one of the M6800 packages under the type number M6820. The M6821 is almost identical as far as the user is concerned, but has slightly different internal logic and some functional improvements.

In the M6820 the registers are all cleared when $\overline{\text{Reset}}$ goes low, but the flag bits can be set even though $\overline{\text{Reset}}$ is low if the control inputs have a high to low transition. In the M6821 all bits are held at 0 while $\overline{\text{Reset}}$ is low, regardless of the signals applied to the control inputs. The enable input of the M6821 has a lower input capacitance than that of the M6820 (7.5 pF compared with 20 pF) and greater noise margins.

The most significant change is probably in the output drive rating. This has been increased from 1 TTL load for the M6820 to 2 TTL loads for the M6821. This applies to both the data ports PA and PB and to the interrupt request lines IRQA and IRQB.

The M6821 has two ports, each of which has three registers accessible to the programmer. For port A these are

$$
\begin{array}{lll}
\text{CRA} & - & \text{control register A} \\
\text{DDRA} & - & \text{data direction register A} \\
\text{PA} & - & \text{data register A}
\end{array}
$$

The second or port B has three similar registers CRB, DDRB and PB. Each wire of each port can be programmed as either an input or an output by putting a 0 or a 1 in the corresponding bit position of the data direction register. This state can be changed at any time by appropriate instructions, but to take advantage of the facility the external connection must be bidirectional.

The data port is normally written to or read from a byte at a time via the data bus. The control register includes some flag bits which are read-only, together with write-only control bits which command the functions of the package.

The package has 40 pins, and since it must use 10 (8 data and 2 control) for each port, 8 for the data lines, 3 chip select inputs, etc., only 2 pins are available for register selection. Consequently only 4 different addresses can be used and, with 6 registers requiring access, the data port and the data direction register share the same address. The choice between the two is made by means of bit 2 in the control register. To the user, the registers are thus accessed as shown in figure 3.1.

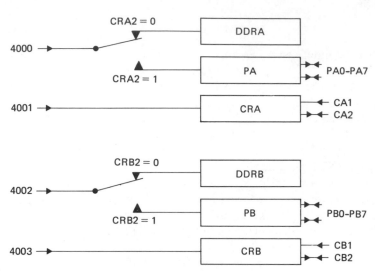

Figure 3.1 Access to registers of M6821

The connections to the processor are as follows:

D0–D7	Data lines to data bus
CS0, CS1, $\overline{\text{CS2}}$	Three chip select lines – CS1 and CS2 active high, $\overline{\text{CS2}}$ active low
RS0, RS1	Register select lines
R/W	Read/write
CE	Chip enable
$\overline{\text{Reset}}$	Clears all registers to zero (active low)
$\overline{\text{IRQA}}$, $\overline{\text{IRQB}}$	Interrupt request lines, active low

The three chip select lines are usually connected to address lines, perhaps using additional decoding to select one from a number of PIAs, as shown in figure 2.2. The chip enable line is usually connected to Ø2, or Ø2. VMA, if the VMA signal has not been gated in elsewhere. VMA signifies that the information on the address lines is a valid address which may be decoded. At certain times in the processor cycle the address lines indicate the contents of the index register or the stack pointer. VMA is low at these times, so ensuring that these register contents are not interpreted as addresses.

$\overline{\text{Reset}}$ is connected to the $\overline{\text{Reset}}$ pin of the CPU and is held low for a few milliseconds when power is applied to the system, so clearing the six registers in the PIA. This ensures that any apparatus connected to the PIA is initially set to a known state, which should always be designed to ensure safe operation. Thus any electric motor controller would start with the motor unenergised, and only after carrying out checks for obstruction, safety, etc., would the motor be gradually energised and allowed to build up to its normal speed.

The two $\overline{IRQ}$ lines are open-drain outputs, active low, and are usually both connected to the processor $\overline{IRQ}$ line. If fast interrupt handling and priority arbitration is important, they can be taken separately to a priority arbitration package. This assesses the highest priority request and sends its vector address from a small ROM to the processor. For smaller systems the most important line could be connected to the $\overline{NMI}$ input which the processor treats as higher priority than the $\overline{IRQ}$ line.

The external connections to the PIA are

PA0–PA7	8 data lines, port A
CA1, CA2	control lines, port A
PB0–PB7	8 data lines, port B
CB1, CB2	control lines, port B

The data lines have bistables driving them when they are programmed as outputs, so that data, once written to them by the processor, are stored unchanged until altered by the next write operation. Control lines CA1 and CB1 are always inputs, but CA2 and CB2 can be programmed to be either inputs or outputs.

The two control registers act in identical ways on the A and B ports, and the action of the individual bits in CRA is as follows, for CA2 as input.

Bit	Action
CRA0	Controls CA1 interrupt, 0 = disable, 1 = enable
CRA1	Controls active transition of CA1, = 1 for 1 → 0, = 0 for 1 → 0
CRA2	Controls access to DDRA or PA, = 0 for DDRA, = 1 for PA
CRA3	Controls CA2 interrupt, 0 = disable, 1 = enable
CRA4	Controls active transition of CA2, = 0 for 1 → 0, = 1 for 1 → 0
CRA5	Controls direction of CA2, = 0 for input
CRA6	CA2 flag (read only)
CRA7	CA1 flag (read only)

The format is shown in figure 3.2.

A somewhat unusual feature of CRA6 and CRA7 is that they are read-only bits for the processor. In order to clear them after an interrupt, the processor must read data from the data register PA. If PA is programmed as an input this read operation will probably occur during the interrupt service routine; other-

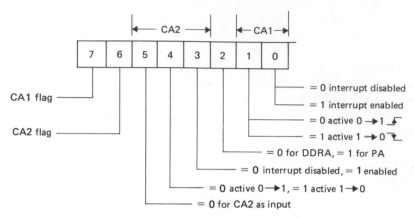

Figure 3.2 Operation of control register CRA with CA2 as input (CRA5 = 0)

wise the flags can be cleared by a 'dummy' read for the purpose, in which the incoming data are ignored.

When CA2 is required as an output, usually to signal to the external device that the processor has sent a byte of data which it can use, CRA5 is programmed to be 1.

If CRA4 is 0, CA2 is cleared to 0 on the negative-going transition of CE after a processor read operation on PA. If CRA3 is 0, CA2 is set when the flag CRA7 is set. If CRA3 is 1, CA2 is set by the first negative-going edge of CE which occurs as the three CS signals are being removed.

If CRA4 is 1, CA2 copies the data sent to CRA3 by the processor.

The B port and its control lines CB1 and CB2 operate in almost exactly the same way as the A port, except that CB2 is cleared when CRB4 is 0 by a write to PB.

Electrically the ports PA and PB differ in that port A is intended for input and has internal pull-up resistors which set any disconnected bit to logic 1. Switches can be connected directly to the port with no additional components by arranging that a logic 0 input shorts the port lines to earth.

Port B is intended as output and has tri-state drives. These give equal driving current for positive-going and negative-going transitions, but when the port acts as input the tri-state driver is high impedance. There is no pull-up resistor, so any input circuit must contain its own source of e.m.f., or, if a sensing switch or relay contacts, must have external pull-up resistors.

3.2 Programming the M6821

To illustrate how the M6821 PIA can be controlled by program we assume that it is connected to the address bus using the following locations

Port A data/DDR   4000
Port A control register   4001
Port B data/DDR   4002
Port B control register   4003

When power is first applied to the microprocessor the start-up circuit will generate a $\overline{\text{Reset}}$ pulse which clears all registers. Thus the first byte sent to locations 4000 and 4002 will load the data direction registers. To access the data ports PA and PB the bits CRA2 and CRB2 of the two control registers must be set.

The initial clear of DDRA and DDRB will program ports A and B both as inputs. Should for example port B be required to act as an output port, the contents of DDRB must be changed to eight 1's, or FF in hexadecimal. The simplest procedure for this is the complement instruction, that is

Machine code

	73
COM 4002	40
	02

Note that this is 1's complement, not the arithmetic 2's complement, better called negate. If however, we require to set for example bits PB0–PB3 as inputs, and PB4–PB7 as outputs we must use an immediate load instruction.

The contents of DDRB must be in binary

1 1 1 1   0 0 0 0

or in hexadecimal F0.

Thus the instructions needed are:

Instruction	*Machine code*	*Action*
LDA A # F0	86	Load F0
	F0	into ACC A
STA A 4002	B7	Copy into
	40	DDR B
	02	

If now we require PA to use both control lines as inputs, active on the positive pulse edge, and allow CA1 to create an interrupt but CA2 merely to set a flag, we need the following bit pattern in CRA

CRA0	=	1 enable IRQA interrupt line
CRA1	=	1 CA1 active on positive edge
CRA2	=	1 next input from 8004 reads from PA
CRA3	=	0 CA2 cannot cause interrupt
CRA4	=	1 CA2 active on positive pulse edge
CRA5	=	0 CA2 is input
CRA6 ⎱		read only, output bits can both be
CRA7 ⎰		zero

The byte sent to CRA must thus be

0 0 0 1   0 1 1 1   or 17 hexadecimal

The program for setting up CRA is thus

Instruction	*Machine code*	*Action*
LDA A # 17	86	Loads 17
	17	into ACC A
STA A 4001	B7	Copies data
	40	into CRA
	01	

Generally the loading of data direction registers and control registers occurs at the beginning of the program, before any external activity has occurred, and their contents are not changed subsequently. This is not essential however, and any port line can be changed from input to output during the execution of the program if the external circuit is designed suitably. One simple example is a manual push-button used to request some activity which cannot be undertaken immediately, such as calling a lift to a particular floor. It is customary to acknowledge the call by means of a lamp which stays alight until the lift reaches the floor and the call is cancelled.

A simple circuit which will meet these conditions is shown in figure 3.3. The line PA1 is initially programmed as an input and is regularly tested by the program. It will be read as logic 1 before the button is pressed, being held at +5 V by a pull-up resistor in the PIA. As soon as the program detects logic 0 on PA1 it is changed to an output and logic 0 is sent to it so illuminating the LED. This remains lit until the floor is reached and the call is cancelled. The line is then changed back to an input and scanning is resumed. Should a more powerful lamp be required than can be driven by a port output line, a pnp emitter follower could be interposed as shown in figure 3.4.

Although the inclusion of a data direction register allows each line of a port to be programmed individually as input or output, the instruction set does not directly allow any bit of a word to be controlled separately, and setting and

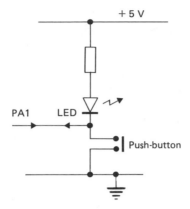

Figure 3.3 Bidirectional line to PIA

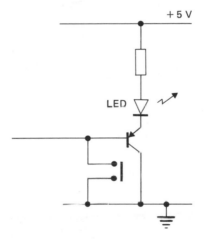

Figure 3.4 Bidirectional line with emitter follower

clearing it can be done only by using a mask and a logical instruction. This is a somewhat clumsy operation, but one which is frequently needed for control applications.

Other microprocessors have provisions for controlling individual bits either through the PIA (Intel 8255) or using processor instructions (8048 family, 8035, 8748, 8021, etc.).

3.3 Flag Testing

Where possible CA1 or CB1 should be used for inputs which require flags to be tested by program. This is because these lines set the MS bit of the control register, which can be tested by a simple sign test, whereas CA2 and CB2 set bit 6. In order to sense this bit all other bits read from the control register must be masked out. The instructions needed for testing flag 1 (CA1) are

Instruction		Code	Action
LOOP :	LDA A 4001	B6	Fetch copy
		40	of CRA
		01	
	BGE LOOP	2C	Branch back
		FC	if CRA7 = 0

Here the load accumulator instruction sets the N and Z bits of the condition code register if the byte loaded represents a negative number (CRA7 = 1), or zero (all bits = 0). This information is used by the 'Branch if greater than or equal to zero' instruction to keep the program in the loop until CA1 is energised.

However, if CA2 is used for the same purpose, a longer program is needed as flag 2 (CRA6) cannot be tested in the presence of other 1's. The program could be as follows

Instruction		Code	Action
LOOP :	LDA A 4001	B6	Fetch copy
		40	of CRA
		01	
	AND A 40	84	Select flag bit
		40	CRA6
	BEQ LOOP	27	Branch back if
		F9	CRA6 = 0

Here the AND instruction uses the mask 0100 0000, so clearing all bits except CRA6 which is unaltered. The next instruction keeps the program in the loop until CRA6 = 1.

The above programs are suitable if the control algorithm requires the program to poll the flag bit until it is set, then continue.

However, if the program is to be held in a larger loop, polling a number of flags in turn, the program would need to continue if the flag were not set, and to branch to some service routine if it were set. In this case the first program could be

Instruction	Code	Action
LDA A 4001	B6	Fetch copy
	40	of CRA
	01	
BMI SERV 1	2B	Branch to service
	XX	routine 1 if CRA7=1

The program for CA2 would require a branch instruction

            BNE SERV 2   26
                                          XX

to make it branch to the service routine SERV 2 if CRA6 = 1, otherwise carrying on to the next test.

3.4   Interrupt Handling with the M6821 PIA

The M6800 microprocessor has two interrupt request lines, $\overline{\text{IRQ}}$ and $\overline{\text{NMI}}$. The $\overline{\text{NMI}}$ (non-maskable interrupt) has the higher priority and is generally reserved for fast devices requiring prompt attention. It is always serviced immediately after the current instruction has been executed.

The PIA is usually connected to the $\overline{\text{IRQ}}$ line, having an open-drain FET driver. The $\overline{\text{IRQ}}$ line has a pull-up resistor inside the processor package, but if many packages are connected to it, an external 3.3 kΩ resistor to +5 V will give more reliable operation.

The $\overline{\text{IRQ}}$ line is controlled by the interrupt mask of I bit or the condition code register (bit CCR4) which can be set or cleared by the instructions SEI (disable interrupt) or CLI (enable interrupt). It is initially set by the reset operation after power has been applied, and is also set immediately an interrupt sequence has been started. This is done automatically by the processor and no program instruction is required. Note that setting the I bit disables interrupts.

Local control of the PIA interrupts is obtained via bits 0 and 3 of the control register. Initially these are cleared, so preventing interrupts via the control lines. If interrupts are required, these bits must be changed to 1.

The M6800 has a simple form of interrupt vectoring which provides a single address for all $\overline{\text{IRQ}}$ interrupts. The processor reads the address held in locations FFF8 and FFF9 and takes this as the starting address of the service routine. Should more than one device be permitted to interrupt the processor, the first part of the program must be a flag-testing sequence to determine which device created the interrupt, and hence which service routine to execute. Each PIA can deal with four sources of interrupts if all of the control lines are programmed as inputs. There are two $\overline{\text{IRQ}}$ outputs from the PIA, one for each port, and they are normally both connected to the $\overline{\text{IRQ}}$ line of the processor.

If, for example, port A were connected to the peripheral which needed the fastest response, its interrupt line $\overline{\text{IRQA}}$ could be connected to $\overline{\text{NMI}}$ to give it automatic priority over any $\overline{\text{IRQ}}$ request. The processor would then read locations FFFC and FFFD to find the starting address of the $\overline{\text{NMI}}$ service routine, and locations FFF8 and FFF9 for the starting address of the $\overline{\text{IRQ}}$ service routine.

The service routine is simpler to write than for many other microprocessors, since there is no need to program the saving and restoring of the processor register contents.

As part of the initial interrupt sequence, before beginning the service routine, the processor automatically saves on the stack the contents of all registers apart from the stack pointer. At the end of the routine the single instruction RTI causes a return to the main program, and automatically restores the contents of the processor registers.

A simple example of an interrupt service routine is shown below. This reads a byte of data from a port at address 4000, stores it in location 0010 and then sends it out to a lamp display at location 4002 for the operator to check.

Instruction		*Code*	*Action*
ECHO :	LDA A 4000	B6 40 00	Fetch data byte
	STA A 10	97 10	Copy into location 10
	STA A 4002	B7 40 02	Output to lamps
	CLI	0E	Enable interrupt
	RTI	3B	Return to main program

Pin connections for the M6821 and other packages in the M6800 family are given in Appendix C.

3.5   The Intel 8255 PPI

The Intel Programmable Peripheral Interface is intended for use with the 8080 and 8085 microprocessor families. It is broadly similar to the M6820 but has 24 pins available for connecting to external devices in place of the 20 of the M6820. The I/O pins are divided into three 8-bit ports, A, B and C, with port C being divided into an upper and a lower half.

Using a 40-pin package there are 24 pins used for the ports, 8 for the data bus, 4 for control lines $\overline{RD}$, $\overline{WR}$, $\overline{CS}$ and RESET, so leaving only two for address lines. Thus only four device codes or addresses can be used, and as there are five registers to be accessed, some additional decoding is needed. This is done by using one address for both control and bit set/reset registers, the selection being made by bit 7 of the byte sent to them. As these registers are both write-only, this causes no difficulty. There are no data direction registers, but the four parts of ports A, B and C can be set for input or output independently. The direction of data flow is determined by the $\overline{\text{WR}}$ or $\overline{\text{RD}}$ lines, only one of which is active at a time. For a **PPI** connected to respond to device codes 10–13 the access arrangements for the programmer would be as shown in figure 3.5.

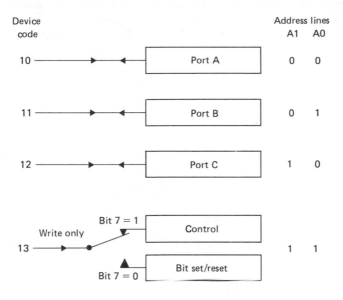

Figure 3.5 Access to registers of 8255 PPI

The instruction

OUT 10 would then copy the contents of the accumulator into port A, and

IN 11 could copy the data presented to port B into the accumulator.

The $\overline{\text{RD}}$ and $\overline{\text{WR}}$ signals combine the functions of the R/W, VMA and Ø2 clock of the M6800, and have the logical equivalence

$$\overline{\text{RD}} = \overline{(\text{R/W} \cdot \text{VMA} \cdot \text{Ø2})}$$

and $\qquad \overline{\text{WR}} = \overline{(\overline{\text{R/W}} \cdot \text{VMA} \cdot \text{Ø2})}$

These signals provide timing for the data transfer and obviate the need to distribute a Ø2 clock signal.

When power is initially applied to the processor, a reset signal is required to start program execution. This is also sent to the PPI and resets all registers so that all three ports behave as inputs.

The way in which the ports operate is controlled by writing to the control register, selected by an address which has the two LS bits both set, so that A0 and A1 are both high. The chip select pin $\overline{CS}$ must be low, and this is usually connected to some decoding logic which ensures that the PPI address does not conflict with the addresses of other packages connected to the address bus. Also $\overline{WR}$ will be pulsed low by the CPU transfer data from the data lines to the control register.

The various bits of the control register act as follows

Bit no.	Controls	Action
CR0	Port C low half (PC0–PC3)	1 = input, 0 = output
CR1	Port B	1 = input, 0 = output
CR2	Mode of port B and port C low half	0 = mode 0, 1 = mode 1
CR3	Port C upper half (PC4–PC7)	1 = input, 0 = output
CR4	Port A	1 = input, 0 = output
CR5/CR6	Mode of port C upper half and port A	00 = mode 0, 01 = mode 1 1 X = mode 2
CR7	Must be 1 to select control register	0 will select bit set/reset register

The modes which can be programmed are

Mode 0	Basic input/output
Mode 1	Strobed input/output
Mode 2	Bidirectional bus (port A only)

Mode 0 corresponds to the action of the M6821 in that the output byte is latched but the input is not latched. In mode 1 both input and output are latched, ports A and B being used for data and port C for control. In mode 2 port A can be used as an 8-bit bidirectional bus, with latched inputs and outputs. Five bits of port C are used for control.

The facility for creating an interrupt with the 8255 is markedly different from that of the M6821 in that the package has no INTR pin which is connected directly to the microprocessor. Interrupts can be set up conveniently in modes 1 and 2 by connecting PC3 (port A) or PC0 (port B) to the processor INTR pin. An interrupt enable/disable bistable INTE is included on the 8255 which is controlled by setting or resetting one of the port C lines. The control lines are allocated as follows

Control functions		*Port*	
		A	B
Input	$\overline{\text{STB}}$	PC4	PC2
	IBF	PC5	PC1
	INTR	PC3	PC0
Output	$\overline{\text{OBF}}$	PC7	PC1
	$\overline{\text{ACK}}$	PC6	PC2
	INTR	PC3	PC0

For input, if the INTE bistable is set, interrupts are accepted, and the sequence is

(1) data are presented to the port
(2) $\overline{\text{STB}}$ is pulsed low, so loading the data into the input latch
(3) IBF is set when $\overline{\text{STB}}$ goes low, to acknowledge receipt of the data
(4) when IBF is set, the INTR output goes high when $\overline{\text{STB}}$ returns to high, so creating a processor interrupt
(5) when the processor reads the data by sending an $\overline{\text{RD}}$ signal, IBF is reset and INTR is reset

For an interrupt operation the three port C lines are designated as follows

$\overline{\text{OBF}}$ A flag which indicates that the processor has loaded data into the output latch. It changes to logical 0 on the trailing edge of $\overline{\text{WR}}$ and returns high on the leading edge of $\overline{\text{ACK}}$.

$\overline{\text{ACK}}$ A signal sent to the 8255 by the peripheral to signify that it has read the data.

INTR If INTE is enabled, and $\overline{\text{OBP}}$ has returned to logic 1, the INTR output will be set by $\overline{\text{ACK}}$ returning to logic 1 and cleared by the next $\overline{\text{WR}}$ pulse.

In mode 2 the bits of port C behave in an identical manner for the bidirectional port A, but the remaining pins can be used separately as either output or input lines.

In order to control individual bits of port C, when programmed for output, the bit set/reset function is selected by writing to the control register address (A0 = A1 = 1) but with bit 7 = 0.

The other digits of the byte act as follows

D0	selected bit is set (D0 = 1) or cleared (D0 = 0)
D1, D2, D3	contain an octal number (MSB is D3) which selects the required bit of port C
D4, D5, D6	are 'don't care' inputs

3.6 Programming the 8255

As an example we consider a PPI which is connected to the address lines so that it uses the four device codes 10, 11, 12, 13 (hexadecimal). If the CPU is an 8080, the signals which indicate an I/O transfer are obtained by latching the status from the data lines at an early phase of instruction execution. The time is defined by a SYNC pulse from the CPU and a special 8228 system controller package is provided which performs this function and also buffers the data lines. The $\overline{\text{IN}}$ or $\overline{\text{I/OR}}$ (I/O read) signal is obtained from data line 4 and the $\overline{\text{OUT}}$ or $\overline{\text{I/OW}}$ (I/O write) from data line 6. These are connected to the $\overline{\text{RD}}$ and $\overline{\text{WR}}$ pins of the PPI and are active low. The CS pin can be used for addressing the PPI and may need only to be connected via an inverter to one of the higher-order device code (address) lines if no more than four I/O packages are used.

The available addresses would select PPI registers as follows

Device code 10   Port A
Device code 11   Port B
Device code 12   Port C
Device code 13   Control or bit set/reset (write only)

Thus, assuming that the system has just been reset, the control register must first be loaded, then data can be transferred to or from the ports. The required bit pattern is assembled in the accumulator by a Move immediate instruction and then output to the PPI. The program used could be as given below:

Instruction	*Code*	*Action*
MVI A # B1	3E	Assembles bit pattern
	B1	in ACC
OUT 13	D3	Output to
	13	control register

The binary pattern output is

B	1
1011	0001

Starting with the bit D0 on the right, the significance of each bit is

D0 = 1	Lower-order bits of port C are inputs
D1 = 0	Port B is output
D2 = 0	Port B is in mode 0
D3 = 0	High-order bits of port C are outputs
D4 = 1	Port A is input
D5 = 1, D6 = 0	Port A is in mode 1
D7 = 1	Needed to obtain access to control register

In this case not all the bits of port C are available for independent use, since PC3, PC4 and PC5 are needed for the INTR, $\overline{\text{STB}}$ and IBF signals as port A is programmed for strobed input.

We could subsequently write to port B by the instruction

OUT 11

This would copy the byte in the accumulator via the data lines to port B.

Similarly

IN 10

would read the data sent to port A and transfer it to the accumulator.

As another example, if the pattern

90 hexadecimal = 1001 0000 binary

were sent to the control register, the change from the previous example would be that port A is set at mode 0, freeing PC3, PC4, PC5, and both halves of port C are set for output.

If this port were then used to control for example a set of alarm lamps, the bit set/reset feature would allow independent control of each lamp. If, for example, we required to turn on the lamp connected to PC2 (bit 2 of port C) by setting it, the program would be

Instruction	*Code*	*Action*
MVI A, # 05	3E	Set up bit pattern
	05	in ACC
OUT 13	D3	Output to bit set/reset
	13	register

The byte output to the register is

0000   0101

Starting with D0 on the right, the digits act as follows:

D0	1 to set the selected line
D1, D2, D3	Contain 010 to select line PC2
D4, D5, D6	'Don't care' values coded as zero
D7	0 to select bit set/reset register

The same program with pattern 04 would clear PC2, so turning off the lamp.

This program is shorter than the corresponding one for the M6800, but needs a set of 16-bit patterns to be stored and accessed by an indexed instruction if any one of the lamps is to be turned on or off by the same section of program.

3.7   Serial Interfaces for the M6800

Two packages are provided for the M6800 family of microprocessors; the M6850 Asynchronous Communications Interface Adapter (ACIA) and the M6852 Synchronous Serial Data Adapter (SSDA). They are both capable of full duplex working and are designed to connect directly to the data bus, and transfer a byte in parallel to or from the processor. The M6850 has only four registers which act as follows.

Transmit Data Register (TDR)   When data are sent from the processor to this register it will be stored if a previous character is still being transmitted, otherwise it will be sent immediately.

Receive Data Register (RDR)   If this register is empty, a character which has been received by the shift register will automatically be transferred to it.

Control Register (CR)   This is a write-only register whose contents control the division rate between the transmitter clock and the transmitter bit rate, the choice of 7 or 8 data bits, a parity bit, one or two stop bits and the ability of the receiving and transmitting sides to create interrupts.

Status Register (SR)   This is a read-only register which signals on the individual bits

   that the RDR is full (SR0)

   that the TDR is empty (SR1)

   that no carrier is reaching the modem from the remote terminal (SR2)

   that a clear-to-send signal has been received from the modem (SR3)

   a framing error (incorrect framing of data bits between start and stop
      bits) (SR4)

   receiver overrun — an error caused by failure to read one character before the
      next character overwrites it (SR5)

parity error in received character (SR6)

interrupt request — this bit signals when an interrupt has been requested (SR7)

Although containing four registers, the ACIA has only one register select line; the other selection is performed by the R/W line as shown below

RS	R/W	Register selected
0	0	Control
0	1	Status
1	0	Transmit data
1	1	Receive data

Typical addressing arrangements are shown in figure 3.6

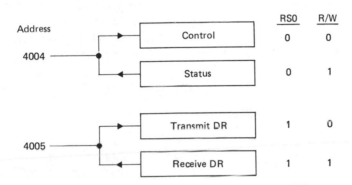

Figure 3.6 Access to registers of 6850 ACIA

For many applications the interface is connected directly to a teleprinter or VDU, and the output is controlled directly by the microprocessor. The only action then required is to test whether the transmit buffer is empty; if so, a character can be sent to the ACIA, if not, the processor is held in a waiting loop. The processor is generally concerned with outputting a message which has previously been loaded into the store, and it can output the successive characters of the message much faster than the teleprinter or VDU can accept them.

If the processor is heavily loaded it may have to perform other tasks while waiting to output the next character. In such cases the flag which signifies that a character is required can also be arranged to create an interrupt. The service routine then outputs a character, decrements a character count, and returns to the main program.

Before using the ACIA its control register must be set up. This is accessed at the lower of the two addresses used (RS = 0).

The 8 bits are divided into 4 fields, which control the ACIA as follows

CR1	CR0	Function
0	0	1
0	1	16
1	0	64
1	1	Master reset

These bits control the divider which couples the transmit and receive clock inputs to the bit rate generator. For many applications a ratio of ÷ 16 is used, as this (and the ÷ 64) do not require the receive clock to be synchronised with the receive data stream. The master reset must be programmed after the reset pulse has been sent to the computer when the power is applied. The control register can then be loaded for the functions required.

Bits CR2, CR3 and CR4 are the word select bits which determine the word length, type or parity check and the number of stop bits, according to the table

CR4	CR3	CR2	No. of data bits	Parity	Stop bits
0	0	0	7	even	2
0	0	1	7	odd	2
0	1	0	7	even	1
0	1	1	7	odd	1
1	0	0	8	—	2
1	0	1	8	—	1
1	1	0	8	even	1
1	1	1	8	odd	1

When the ACIA is connected to a modem for transmitting data via a telephone channel, it is normal practice to check that the circuit is operative before sending data. To effect this, the sending terminal emits a 'request to send' signal; if the line is working the receiving terminal will return a 'clear to send' signal. The receiving terminal can also monitor the state of the line during the transmission since the modem emits a 'data carrier detect' signal. Any break in the telephone circuit will interrupt the carrier tones and the 'data carrier detect' signal will indicate this.

The request to send ($\overline{\text{RTS}}$) signal is controlled by bits 5 and 6 of the control register, which also control the transmit interrupt feature. The four options are:

CR6	CR5	Function ·
0	0	$\overline{RTS}$ low, interrupt disabled
0	1	$\overline{RTS}$ low, interrupt enabled
1	0	$\overline{RTS}$ high, interrupt disabled
1	1	$\overline{RTS}$ low, interrupt disabled
		Transmits a break signal on transmit data output

The 'break' signal is a continuous space signal which is often used to enable a terminal to call a processor and request service.

The last (MS) bit, CR7, if set enables an interrupt to be signalled for any of the following states of the receiving channel

Receive data register full
Overrun
Low to high transition on the $\overline{DCD}$ (data carrier detect) signal line

As an example of programming the ACIA, the following program segment could be used to initialise the device after power-up. We assume that the two addresses used are 4004 (control/status) and 4005 (transmit and receive data). The program must first set bits 0 and 1 of the control register, to reset the ACIA. The required byte can then be sent to the same register to set the conditions needed.

Instruction	Code	Action
LDA A # 03	86 03	Set bits 0 and 1 in ACC A
STA A 4004	B7 40 04	Transfer to control register
LDA A # 05	86 05	Load bit pattern into ACC A
STA A 4004	B7 40 04	Transfer to control register

The control byte used here, 05, will set the following conditions

CR1, CR0	Clock ÷ 16
CR4, CR3, CR2	7 data bits, odd-parity bit, 2 stop bits
CR6, CR5	$\overline{RTS}$ low, transmit interrupt disabled
CR7	Receive interrupt disabled

In order to output a character which we assume has been loaded into accumulator B, we read the status register contents into accumulator A and then test bit 1 (transmit data register empty). If this is set, we output the character to the transmit data register; if not, the test is repeated until the current character has been sent, and TDRE is sent.

Instruction	*Code*	*Action*
→TEST : LDA A 4004	B6	Copy status register
	40	into ACC A
	04	
AND A #02	84	Isolate bit 1
	02	
BEQ TEST	27	Branch back to
	F9	test if clear
STA B 4005	F7	TDR empty, send
	40	character to transmit
	05	data register

As with the PIA, the status bit which signifies that TDR is empty is read only, so that it cannot be controlled directly by program. It is automatically cleared by the last instruction, which writes the character into the transmit data register.

The receiving channel is programmed in a similar manner, but bit 0 of the status register is tested to determine whether the receive data register is full, indicating that a character is available for reading.

There is an important matter to note when programming the ACIA; since there are two registers which can be accessed at each address, selected by the R/W signal, some instructions cannot be used. These involve operations in which data are read from a register, modified by the CPU and then written back into the register. Examples are COM (complement), INC (increment) and DEC (decrement). These will give unpredictable results because they will read from one register, that is, the status register, and write back into another register, in this case the control register.

The same warning applies to the SSDA, and to the USART when its address is memory-mapped.

3.8   The Intel 8251A USART

This device (Universal Synchronous or Asynchronous Receiver/Transmitter) can operate either in synchronous or asynchronous mode. It has a single chip select input for addressing which must be low for the device to operate, and a single register select line (here called C/$\overline{D}$) which selects either the control and status registers, or the data registers. The $\overline{RD}$ and $\overline{WR}$ signals are also used to determine which of the register pairs is accessed, in the same way as the R/W line is used in the M6850. The signals needed to access the various registers are shown in figure 3.7.

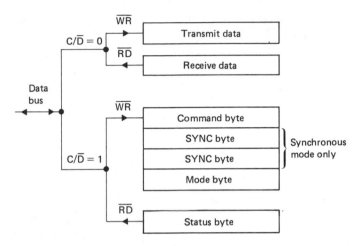

Figure 3.7 Registers of 8251 USART

The 8251A operates in an almost identical fashion to the M6821 for asynchronous working, but in order to handle the synchronous mode as well, it has an additional mode register. In order to allow the receiving terminal to decide where the boundaries of the bytes are in a continuous stream of data, the transmitting terminal sends out one or two bytes of an agreed synchronising character (SYNC). The USART must be programmed to operate with either one or two SYNC characters which are automatically inserted by the transmitter before any data bytes are sent. Since synchronisation depends upon a continuous bit stream, should the transmitting microprocessor fail to send data to the USART, it will automatically insert SYNC characters until more data arrive. These and the initial SYNC characters are stripped off by the receiving USART and only the data bytes reach the terminal or processor.

Initially the microprocessor sends a mode byte to the USART which indicates the particular transmission characteristics required as follows:

D1, D0	Must be both 0 for synchronous mode
D3, D2	Indicate 5, 6, 7 or 8 data bits (00 = 5, 11 = 8)
D4	Set to 1 to insert a parity bit
D5	1 for even, 0 for odd parity
D6	1 for external, 0 for internal synchronising detection (SYNDET)
D7	1 for single SYNC, 0 for double SYNC character

The mode byte indicates to the USART whether synchronous or asynchronous working is required by means of bits D1 and D0. These are both 0 for synchronous operation, but for asynchronous operation they are coded 01, 10 or 11 for a clock division ratio of $\div 1$, $\div 16$ or $\div 64$. The remaining bits act in the same way as for synchronous operation, except that D7 and D6 are encoded as 01, 10 or 11 to provide 1, 1½ or 2 stop bits.

For asynchronous working only one mode byte is required; this is followed by a command instruction byte and then by data bytes.

For synchronous working, the mode byte is followed by one or two SYNC bytes which are stored within the USART. SYNC characters are transmitted at the start of a message, and are used in the hunt mode when searching for a match with incoming SYNC bytes.

The format for a particular message is shown in figure 3.8 using either synchronous or asynchronous operation.

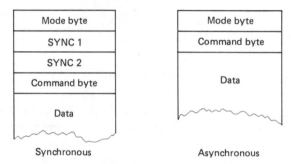

Figure 3.8 Typical data block for 8251 USART

The final character is a command instruction byte which can clear error flags, enable or disable interrupts, control $\overline{\text{RTS}}$ and reset the USART so that it returns to await a new mode byte. The MS bit at the receiving terminal is initially set at 1 to enter the hunt mode. This looks for a match between the incoming bit stream and the SYNC character already loaded. The receiving shift register is initially loaded with all 1's. When one or two SYNC characters have been detected (depending on the MS bit of the mode byte), the SYNDET line is driven high. This indicates to the processor that data characters are being assembled, so that it must await an RXRDY (receiver ready) signal which will denote that a character is ready to read. When this occurs bit 1 of the status register is set. This can be sensed by polling or it can be arranged to cause an interrupt.

Similarly when the transmitting channel is ready for another character, bit 0 of the status register is set.

The USART will operate at any speed up to 19.2K bauds.

3.9   M6852 Synchronous Serial Data Adapter (SSDA)

This device performs a similar function to that of the USART in synchronous mode, but with some different features. It can handle bit rates up to 600K bauds, and has 3-byte first-in first-out (FIFO) storage in the transmit and receive channels. As with the 6851, there is only one register select input, other selection being performed by the R/W input. The program has access to four registers directly, as shown below

RS	R/W	Register	Access
0	0	Control 1	Write only
0	1	Status	Read only
1	0	Transmit data	Write only
1	1	Receive data	Read only

There are three more write-only registers which are accessed if RS = 1, R/W = 0. The particular register is determined by the contents of bits 6 and 7 of control register 1 (CR1).

The other functions of CR1 are control of transmit and receive interrupts, resetting transmitter and receiver, and stripping or transmission of SYNC characters. One bit also disables the synchronising feature and returns the SSDA to searching for SYNC characters. Control register 2 determines the word size (6, 7 or 8 data bits) and the type of parity, the synchronising match output, and whether two bytes can be transferred in succession without checking the FIFO buffer state.

Control register 3 controls the number of SYNC characters used, and whether external or internal synchronising is used, together with the $\overline{CTS}$ (clear to send) modem signal.

The final write-only register is the sync code register. This is loaded with the SYNC character which will be used for transmitting and receiving.

This device can handle data transfers a little faster than earlier devices on account of its 3-byte buffer stores. This enables two bytes to be sent or read in succession without any intervening read from the status register to determine whether data are due for transfer.

This is possible because the transmit and receive flags can be set only when two bytes are ready for reading, or the transmit buffer has space for two bytes.

3.10   Counter/Timer Packages

Counter/timer packages enable time delays to be generated, or events counted without the use of the central processor. Typical of these is the M6840 Programmable Timer Module (PTM) for the Motorola M6800 family of processors.

It has three 16-bit binary counters, three corresponding control registers, a 16-bit buffer register and a status register. Three register select pins are provided. Together with the R/W line these enable 8 read-only registers and 8 write-only registers to be accessed. Since the data path is only 8 bits wide, only 8 bits can be transferred in any operation so that 12 different areas require access to the internal data bus. There is thus some redundancy in the addressing. The various registers accessible to the programmer are shown in figure 3.9.

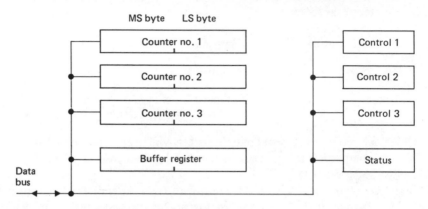

Figure 3.9 Registers of 6840 Programmable Timer Module

Each counter can operate from an external clock or from the system clock. It can be treated as a 16-bit counter, or as two 8-bit counters in cascade. Each counter has an associated latch which can be loaded by the processor. When initialised, this number is transferred to the counter which then counts down to zero, sets a flag, and if so programmed will create an interrupt. This action can be performed once, or repetitively, and an output pin is available which is driven by a bistable triggered when the counter reaches zero. When driven continuously this generates a square wave whose frequency is controlled by the microprocessor.

Other operating modes enable the frequency of a signal or the duration of a pulse to be compared with the number stored in the latch.

Signals derived from the processor are

8 data bits to or from the data bus
Ø2 clock
R/W
3 register select signals for addressing RS0, RS1, RS2
2 chip select inputs $\overline{CS0}$, CS1
$\overline{Reset}$

A single $\overline{IRQ}$ open-drain output is connected to the processor $\overline{IRQ}$ pin.

Each of the three counter/timers has an input for an external clock pulse train, a clock gate enable input, and an output line.

A ÷ 8 prescaler can be inserted into the clock input to timer 3. The maximum input frequency is then 4 MHz for the standard 6840, but 6 or 8 MHz for the A or B versions.

3.11 DMA Controllers

Although interrupts can deal with requests for service fairly quickly, they still require several instructions to transfer one byte from an external device to the data store. Thus in addition to a possible flag-polling routine, each byte transferred may involve the following actions

transfer byte from device to accumulator
transfer byte from accumulator to store
increment store address
decrement byte count
test byte count for zero

The ensuing data transfer rate may be too slow for some applications such as handling fast disc-store transfers or processor-to-processor transfers; for these a procedure called direct memory access (DMA) can be used. This is an autonomous operation in that no program instructions are executed during the transfers, but they are needed for initially loading registers.

Additional hardware is needed for DMA transfers, in which the processor is bypassed and data are interchanged directly between store and peripheral device. The following features are needed

(a) An address register to drive the address lines, normally incremented after each byte has been transferred.

(b) A byte counter register which is decremented after each transfer.

(c) A zero-detecting gate attached to the byte counter register. This signals when the required number of bytes has been transferred, and is usually arranged to interrupt the processor.

(d) Facilities for disabling the address and data line drivers in the processor, and holding up the processor during the transfer.

(e) Address drivers in the DMA interface, and also data line drivers if it is a source of data.

There are two main modes of operation, cycle-stealing and burst mode. In cycle-stealing the processor is held up for only one store cycle at a time. This is the mode generally used when data are being produced rapidly. The alternative is burst mode during which the DMA operation once started continues at the maximum possible rate until all the data have been transferred. This is used when the data have been loaded by some previous action and are all available when the transfer starts.

A typical DMA package is the MC6844 which provides four DMA channels. Each of these has a transfer request line. When one or more request occurs, the highest priority line is selected by a priority arbitration unit, and its number is sent out on two lines TX AKA, TX AKB. A DMA request signal is sent to the clock generator and, at a suitable moment, normally at the beginning of the next processor cycle, a DMA grant is issued. This is connected to the TSC (tri-state control) pin of the processor, so sending the data and address line drivers into the high impedance state.

The same signal is input to the DMAC to notify the selected channel when to output the address required and transfer data, and to drive the R/W line suitably. During the last data transfer the zero-detecting gate is activated and a data end signal is sent to the peripheral.

Three transfer modes are available, TSC steal, Halt steal and Halt burst mode. The first two transfer only a byte at a time, by cycle-stealing. For TSC steal, the clock generator stretches the 01 and 02 clocks during the transfer. For Halt steal the DMA request line is connected to the $\overline{\text{Halt}}$ input to the CPU. When the halt has been allowed by the processor, it issues a bus available (BA) signal which is used as the DMA grant input to the DMAC.

The Halt burst mode operates in a similar fashion, but the halt line is held low until the last byte of the block has been transferred.

In order to provide four separate DMA channels the DMAC must contain a 16-bit address register, a 16-bit byte count register and an 8-bit control register for each of the channels, in addition to an interrupt control register, a priority control register and a data chain register.

The interrupt control register controls whether each channel will create an interrupt when its allocated byte control has been transferred. The priority control register allows each channel to be enabled or disabled, and also for priority rotation. This is a facility for rotating the priority order of the channels so that in the long term each has the same chance of top priority. The data chain register is used to enable the action of one channel working in burst mode to be followed immediately by the transfers programmed into channel 3 (also working in burst mode).

The individual channel control registers provide the following functions

DMA transfer end flag
busy/ready flag
decrement or increment address register, allowing the data block to be accessed from the top or the bottom
whether TSC or Halt control is to be used

whether cycle-stealing or burst mode
read/$\overline{\text{write}}$ to determine the direction of transfer.

To program a DMA channel the following instructions are required

(a) Load the starting address into the address register.
(b) Load the number of bytes to be transferred into the byte counter
register.
Both of these are 16-bit transfers and can normally be done most economically by loading the index register with an immediate operand and then transferring its contents to the DMAC.
(c) Program the read/$\overline{\text{write}}$ bit, the mode bits and the increment/decrement
bit of the channel control register.

The channel is now set up and it can be allowed to start transfers by setting
the required channel bit in the priority control register.
For a processor using a 1 MHz clock rate the maximum transfer rates are

Halt burst mode	1 μs per byte
Halt cycle-steal mode	5–15 μs per byte
TSC cycle-steal mode	4 μs per byte

The speed in the Halt cycle-steal mode depends upon the particular type
of instruction cycle being executed when the DMA request occurs.
Although little extra logic is needed to attach the DMAC to the microprocessor if its data store comprises static RAM, some extra hardware is needed
if dynamic RAM is used. This is caused by the need to give a request for a store
refresh cycle priority over a DMA request. Thus the DMA request from the
DMAC must be inhibited if a refresh request is also present, and in burst mode
the refresh request has priority over the continuous sequence of DMA transfers.

3.12 Priority Interrupt Controllers

Owing mainly to the limited number of pins available for external connections,
most microprocessors provide only one or two interrupt lines. Thus for other
than quite basic systems, several device interfaces will be attached to the same
interrupt line, and in the case of the Motorola M6800 series only one interrupt
vector address is provided for the IRQ interrupt line. This means that the
interrupt service routine must start with a flag-polling sequence to determine
which device is requesting an interrupt; only then can the program branch to
the correct device service routine. As shown in section 3.3 this may be a rather
protracted process, since the flag bit may have to be masked off before being
tested.

Some microprocessors, however, provide facilities for a limited interrupt vectoring capability. For example in the Intel 8080 a restart (RST) instruction is supplied by the peripheral device requesting an interrupt. The INTA pulse which provides the timing signal for this is obtained from the 8228 system controller and is transmitted in 'daisy-chain' fashion through each interface. Any interface which is requesting an interrupt will block the transmission of this pulse, so that if more than one device is requesting an interrupt the interface nearest to the processor will alone receive the INTA pulse. It uses this to gate on to the data lines a restart instruction. This is a single byte format, with bits D0, D1, D2, D6 and D7 all 1, and D3, D4, D5 encoding a digit N. The value of N determines which vector address the processor selects from which to start the service routine. The options are as follows

N	0	1	2	3	4	5	6	7
Address (hexadecimal)	00	08	10	18	20	28	30	38

This operation code is carefully chosen; the data lines are normally connected to +5 V via 'pull-up' resistors of 3–10 kΩ. Thus only those bits of N which have value 0 need driving circuits connected to the data bus. For example for $N = 2$ (010 binary), D3 = 0, D5 = 0, and all other bits of the restart instruction are 1. Thus only two digit lines drivers are needed.

One arrangement which could be used is shown in figure 3.10. This includes a wired-OR line for interrupts, fed by open-collector or open-drain inverters. If there are not more than 8 devices attached to the line, an 8-way OR gate fed from the Q output of the bistable could be used. The output of the gate would drive the 8080 INT line (active high) directly.

In the absence of an interrupt request, bistable IRQ is cleared, so that $\overline{Q} = 1$, and any interrupt acknowledge signal reaching the interface is sent on down the chain. If however an interrupt has been requested Q = 1, $\overline{Q} = 0$ and the INTA signal is not sent further. The combination of $\overline{Q} = 1$ and INTA is used to drive the number N on to the digit lines.

During this action the processor executes a 'store read' operation, but does not emit the memory read signal from the system controller package, or update the program counter. In effect the restart instruction arrives on the data line as if it were a normal instruction supplied from the program store, but it is actually supplied by the device interface.

For a system which has, say, five devices capable of creating interrupts, each with its own vector address, the logic shown in figure 3.10 is repeated five times. This requires a considerable number of packages and wiring, and a much simpler arrangement is possible using the 8214 Priority Interrupt Controller. This will handle eight inputs, arbitrate in favour of the highest pri-

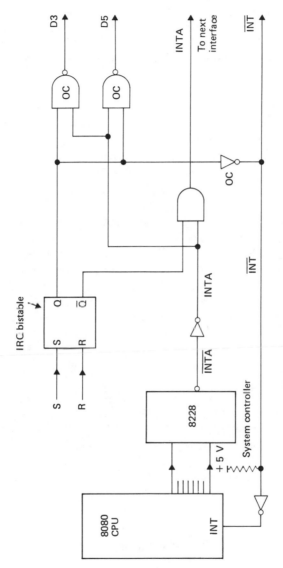

Figure 3.10 Interrupt logic for 8080

ority if more than one is active, and drive the appropriate restart instruction on to the data lines. It also has a status register which can be loaded by program which indicates the priority level assigned to the current routine. Only requests with a higher priority than this will be allowed to interrupt.

The single 8214 thus replaces eight sets of the interrupt logic of figure 3.10, together with a status register and comparator. A further feature is that the 8214 can be cascaded by attaching the output of another 8214 to each input, so providing 64 priority inputs.

When the Intel 8085 was designed some time later, a more complex interrupt package was introduced, which is also compatible with 8080 systems. This is the 8259 Programmable Interrupt Controller. It performs in a similar manner to the 8214 in having eight inputs and a register holding the status of the current routine, but it gives greater flexibility in that the move to the service routine is made by a 'CALL' or 'JUMP TO SUBROUTINE' instruction. This is a 3-byte instruction in which the second and third bytes contain the 16-bit address of the service routine.

As part of the setting-up procedure, registers in the 8259 are loaded with 3 bytes for each input, a command byte and the 2-byte vector address. When the $\overline{\text{INTA}}$ signal arrives from the system controller (8080) or the processor (8085) the 8259 first sends the operation code (CD in hexadecimal) and the next two $\overline{\text{INTA}}$ signals are used to gate the vector address on to the data lines.

This feature allows the service routines to be located anywhere in the address space and yet be reached directly from the interrupt controller.

The Motorola MC6828 Priority Interrupt Controller (PIC) provides facilities similar to those given by the 8214, but the details of the vector address input are rather different on account of the different way the 6800 microprocessor responds to interrupts.

Whereas the 8080 has no 'built-in' vector address, and awaits a restart instruction from the interface, the M6800 has an address built in at which it expects to find the vector address.

In order to supply a separate vector address for each interrupting interface, the PIC must substitute this address for the single address provided by a basic system. This is effected by stretching out the clock pulse so that when the built-in addresses FFF8 and FFF9 are emitted by the processor, the PIC follows these with an address provided by the PIC from a ROM rather than one read from the program store.

As in the 8214, the PIC contains a programmable mask register holding the priority assigned to the current routine, and only if the interrupt request has higher priority is it accepted.

The sequence of operations starts with selection of the line which has the highest active request. This level is compared with that in the mask register, and if it is higher the process continues.

The next stage is a signal to the processor on the IRQ line which begins the interrupt routine. This then puts the address FFF8 on the address lines, a location which should contain the high byte of the vector address. This address is detected by the PIC and it stretches the clock period, so allowing time for a substitute address to be transmitted by the PIC. This substitute address is held in a ROM and is selected by a 4-bit code delivered by the priority decoder. After the high byte of the vector address has been sent the processor sends address FFF9 which is detected by the PIC. Again the clock cycle is stretched, and a substitute low byte of the vector address is read from the ROM and output.

The ROM contains a separate vector address for each device service routine, which must be located in the area FFE8 to FFF9, since the PIC intercepts and modifies only the four low address lines A1, A2, A3 and A4.

The use of the mask register enables each program segment to determine which of the devices will be allowed to interrupt it. In order to detect the two processor addresses FFF8 and FFF9, address lines A5−A15 and VMA are taken to a NAND gate whose output drives the chip select line $\overline{\text{CS0}}$.

3.13   Other Input/Output Packages

As the volume of microprocessor products has increased it has become economic to market more special-purpose packages to control particular devices. Examples of these are controller packages for floppy-disc drives, for video displays, for raster-type CRT displays, and interfaces for keyboard/displays and IEEE 488 bus systems.

For other applications equally complex interfaces can be provided by packages such as the 8041/8741 Universal Peripheral Interface. This has two 8-bit ports for external devices and contains a complete 8-bit microprocessor, together with 1K bytes of program store, 64 bytes of data storage. The 8741 has a user-programmable store, which is UV-erasable, and is intended for system development. For large-volume production the 8041 has a mask ROM which has the program built in at the final stage of manufacture.

Some applications which have been handled by this type of package are keyboard scanning, control of printers and the multiplexing of complicated displays.

Pin connections for the packages in the 8080, 8085 and Z80 families are given in Appendixes A, B and D.

4 Transducers and Signal Conversion

4.1 Signal Transformations for Input and Output

The interface packages described in the previous chapter facilitate the attachment of a range of devices to a microprocessor bus. In general however, other hardware is needed to complete the sometimes lengthy chain of activity between a physical state or quantity which must be measured, and the arrival inside the microprocessor of a numerical representation of that quantity.

The first stage in the measurement of quantities such as force, displacement, velocity, temperature, etc. is the transducer or sensor which generally produces an electrical output representing the variable being measured. Since the input to the microprocessor is in digital form, a transducer which produces a digital output is preferable, but there are many quantities such as temperature which cannot be measured digitally in any convenient way.

In such situations additional units are required which can convert the continuously variable analogue voltage to digital form. Finally it may be necessary to modify the digital signals to suit the voltage levels needed by the interface package.

The final set of operations which involves synchronising the transfer of data to the computer bus with the computer clock timing, and possible data storage and status testing, is most conveniently performed by a parallel I/O package.

Many control applications also require additional devices to be attached to the microprocessor output, to regulate plant and processes, or to control various types of machine. Almost invariably some form of power amplification is required since the microprocessor I/O package can typically handle no more than about 10 mW, whereas many applications require the control of power at the kilowatt level or more.

We first examine the transducers and sensors available for inputting electrical data in digital form.

4.2 Digital Inputs

Many forms of plant and process provide simple binary signals, for example to indicate the following system conditions:

(a) switch open or closed
(b) supply present or not
(c) valve open or closed
(d) tank full or not (from float switch)
(e) material (for example, paper or tape) exhausted (indicated by switch coupled to a spring-loaded sensing arm)
(f) movement reaching a particular position (indicated by a proximity sensor)

Where some mechanical motion is involved it is usually possible to attach a microswitch with an actuator to the mechanism to sense position, for example (c), (d) or (e). Proximity detection can be achieved by capacitance or inductance sensing, or by using a moving magnet and a microswitch or a Hall-effect detector.

Normally eight of these binary inputs are attached to an 8-bit parallel port, and input simultaneously. Any particular line can then be tested either by masking or, if they are available, by bit-testing instructions.

To minimise the number of I/O packages needed in complex systems, the data can be multiplexed. This requires some switching mechanism by which a number of input lines can be connected eight at a time to a particular port input, the selection being controlled by the microprocessor.

For example, if we had 128 binary inputs, these could be connected in groups of eight to sixteen 8-bit gated line buffers. The outputs of all the buffers are connected, in parallel, to an 8-bit I/O port but only one is enabled at a time. Four output lines from the I/O package are needed to select a particular group, by using a 4-input decoder. Each of the sixteen outputs of the decoder is connected to the enable input of a buffer, so that the number output to the decoder determines which group of eight is connected to the port input. The data input process requires first the output of a 4-bit code to select the group, then an input operation from the 8-bit port to read the data from the group. The general arrangement is shown in figure 4.1.

This requires 17 digital packages and half a 24-wire parallel I/O package. The alternative arrangement without multiplexing would require 6 I/O packages and would consequently be more expensive. It would also impose a much greater load on the data bus. This disadvantage of multiplexing is the small increase in access time caused by having to set up the decoder before reading the data.

In a system such as this, input may be reserved for checking purposes, for example sensing the maximum stroke position of an actuator. By commanding a full stroke and measuring the time taken the microprocessor can test that this output device is operating satisfactorily. For other inputs and outputs it may be possible to connect an input to an output and so check the overall operation of both of them.

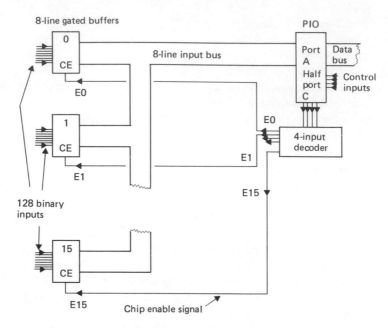

Figure 4.1 Digital multiplexing for 128 binary inputs

4.3 Digital Transducers

Some transducers can produce digital outputs directly, perhaps the simplest being those which generate a stream of pulses, whose number is proportional to the value of the variable being measured. Examples of these are digital flowmeters using either a propeller-type rotor or a displacement system with moving pistons. A low-torque sensing arrangement can be provided either by a magnetic detector or an optical pick-off. A digital signal indicating shaft rotation can also be obtained by using an optical sensor and a disc comprising alternate opaque and transparent bars.

These can be counted to determine angular motion, or the number of pulses generated in a known time can be used to determine angular velocity. A convenient sensor is available comprising a light-emitting diode and a phototransistor moulded into a U-shaped plastic holder. By covering the diode and transistor with a thin layer of plastic and selecting appropriate semiconductors, the sensor can be built to use infra-red radiation, to which the plastic is transparent. The thin layer of plastic prevents visible light from reaching the sensor and so avoids interference from ambient light. Fluorescent tubes are particularly liable to give trouble since they produce 100 bursts of illumination per second. However, direct sunlight does cause trouble since it is accompanied by substantial infra-red radiation. The sensor requires only one resistor to set diode current, and another one to act as load to the phototransistor, together with a 5 V supply, and will produce a volt or two of pulse output.

A pulse output train can also be obtained by mounting a magnetic detector near to a rotating gear wheel. Each tooth then generates a small voltage pulse as it passes the detector. A similar output can be obtained from an a.c. tachogenerator. This is a permanent magnet alternator, and generates an e.m.f. and an output frequency proportional to its angular speed.

If the microprocessor is lightly loaded, the pulse input can be connected to a sense line which sets a flag. The processor is then held in a waiting loop, testing the flag. As soon as this is set, a counter is incremented, the flag is cleared, and the program returns to the waiting loop.

If however the processor must perform other tasks simultaneously, the flag can be arranged to create an interrupt, or a counter/timer chip can be used. This removes all load from the processor, apart from setting up the counter and reading out the final result.

Counting methods of determining angular or linear motion are often used when high resolution (0.001 inch or better) is needed. One scheme uses two optical plates which have a series of parallel lines engraved photographically upon them. One is fixed and the other is attached to the moving part. The gratings are set at a small angle α to one another and in consequence a set of alternately light and dark fringes (called Moiré fringes) appear. These are spaced a distance $d/\tan \alpha \cong d/\alpha$ apart where d is the distance between adjacent lines in the grating, and α the angle of inclination in radians. If α is say 0.01 radian (about ½°), a graticule spacing of 0.001 inch produces light fringes 0.1 inch apart. These are wide enough to be sensed by a photodiode or a phototransistor. The major advantage of this method is that the fringe depends upon a number of ruled lines, so the fringe position depends on the average spacing of a number of lines. One line slightly out of place will produce a very small error.

Normally two optical sensors are provided, spaced at a distance of one-quarter of a fringe apart so that the direction of motion can be determined. This is essential for determining absolute position if the moving grating can move in either direction.

The general appearance of the fringes is shown in figure 4.2. A development

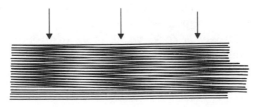

Figure 4.2 Moiré fringes produced by crossed gratings

of the arrangement uses a continuously rotating spiral grating on the moving member and straight ruling on the fixed member. This allows the distance between fringes to be divided into ten or more parts and so increases the resolution of the system.

Absolute position can also be determined by a coded plate. For moderate resolution this can be a printed circuit device with metal brushes to sense the data, but where high resolution is required an optical plate produced photographically is generally used. The principle of all types is that each position of the moving part causes the optical or mechanical sensors to generate a different code pattern. The resolution obtained depends upon the number of tracks used, for example a 12-track system has a resolution of 1 part in 2^{12} or 4096. The signal from each of the tracks is in binary form, but binary coding of the combined signals is not satisfactory. The reason for this is the continuous relative motion of the coded plate and the sensors. If we consider, for example, a three-track system, errors can occur between the two combinations 011 and 100. Owing to the inevitable differences in sensitivity and precise positioning of all three sensors, it is impossible to ensure that the three transitions

D_2	D_1	D_0
0	1	1
↓	↓	↓
1	0	0

will occur simultaneously. Thus between the two correct codes we could momentarily obtain false codes such as

1	1	1
0	0	1
1	0	1
1	1	0
0	0	0

Since the system driving the moving element can generally provide continuous movement, it could stop anywhere between the two correct positions and so indicate a false code output.

The errors can arise only in codes where more than one bit changes value between successive combinations. Thus binary coding is not satisfactory, and a different code is needed in which only a single bit changes value at each step. The normal code which is used to satisfy this need is called the Gray code, after its inventor.

The 4-bit form of the code, and the binary equivalent are given in the table:

Gray code						Binary code			
G_3	G_2	G_1	G_0			B_3	B_2	B_1	B_0
0	0	0	0			0	0	0	0
0	0	0	1			0	0	0	1
0	0	1	1			0	0	1	0
0	0	1	0			0	0	1	1
0	1	1	0			0	1	0	0
0	1	1	1			0	1	0	1
0	1	0	1			0	1	1	0
0	1	0	0			0	1	1	1
1	1	0	0			1	0	0	0
1	1	0	1			1	0	0	1
1	1	1	1			1	0	1	0
		etc.						etc.	

A Gray-coded plate is shown in figure 4.3.

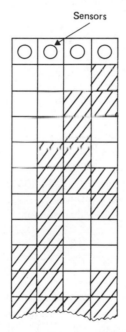

Figure 4.3 Gray-coded plate

The Gray code is sometimes called a 'reflected' code, since the same pattern is found when moving either upwards or downwards from certain points. For example, starting from a point between the fourth and fifth entries, the same pattern of G_0 and G_1 is found when moving in either direction.

The code satisfies the requirement that only one bit changes at a time, but it cannot be used for arithmetic since it does not have constant weighting. This means that 1 in a particular column does not represent a fixed value, as it does in binary code. Consequently when Gray-code input is used, the usual procedure is to convert it immediately into binary form before performing any calculation. This can be done by program, or if conversion time is critical, at greater cost by hardware. Using the 4-bit codes as example, the logical relations between binary and Gray codes are

$$
\begin{aligned}
B_3 &= G_3 \\
B_2 &= B_3 \oplus G_2 \\
B_1 &= B_2 \oplus G_1 \\
B_0 &= B_1 \oplus G_0
\end{aligned}
$$

where $\oplus$ denotes the exclusive-OR functions, or modulus 2 addition, so that

$$
B_3 \oplus G_2 = B_3 \cdot \overline{G_2} + \overline{B_3} \cdot G_2
$$

Many microprocessors include the exclusive-OR function in their instruction sets so simplifying the conversion. In hardware, two quad XOR gate packages will suffice to convert an 8-bit number. Packages available include the 74LS86 (TTL) and the 4070B (CMOS).

Gray-coded plates are available for encoding linear motion, and similarly coded discs can be used for the measurement of angular position.

Other devices which have been used for measuring angular position include inductive and capacitive sensing units. These are not capable of the resolution attainable from optical sensing, but their performance can be improved by using two sensors, one driven directly and the other driven through step-up gearing. The directly driven sensor gives the approximate position, and additional digits are available from the faster sensor.

4.4   Analogue Sensors

There are many more sensors available which provide analogue output signals. For angular or linear position these can be conventional wire-wound potentiometers fed with a constant voltage. The potential of the slider is then a linear function of position. This type suffers from limited resolution since the output is actually a staircase waveform as the slider moves. The height of each step is equal to the voltage between adjacent turns of the potentiometer element. This restriction can be eliminated by using a track of conducting plastic. Other analogue sensors of linear position are inductively coupled units in which the output coil has voltages induced in it by two oppositely wound helical coils. The net output voltage is a linear function of the position of the moving coil.

The same linear sensor could be used to measure the depth of liquid in a tank, by coupling a float to the potentiometer slider, or the moving coil of the inductive sensor.

Force can be measured indirectly by using a strain gauge attached to the machine member carrying the force. The strain gauge is a resistive element (usually a semiconductor) which undergoes a small change in resistance when stretched or compressed. It is usually operated in a bridge circuit, balanced with zero force. The unbalance voltage is then proportional to the strain, that is the relative change in length of the member and the gauge attached to it. Multiplied by Young's modulus, this gives the stress, or force per unit area, in the member, and finally multiplication by the cross-sectional area of the member gives the force. Usually the complete chain is calibrated by putting a known force on the member and observing the corresponding value which reaches the microprocessor. It may be possible to build in an automatic test routine which is executed each time that the processor is switched on. This could either calibrate the force channel automatically or emit a warning and halt the processor if the calibration error were outside the permissible limits.

An alternative method of measuring force involves balancing it with the force exerted by a very linear moving coil actuator. Any change in position is detected by a sensitive optical pick-off whose output is amplified to control the actuator current. The force is then proportional to this current, which can easily be measured digitally. Where it is necessary to display the force, the digital value may be encoded in BCD form.

The pressure difference between two volumes of fluid can be measured by using a flexible metal bellows or a corrugated diaphragm to separate them. The movement of the bellows or diaphragm can be made proportional to the pressure difference, and can be sensed by position transducers.

We have seen that position can be measured by counting pulses from a digital position encoder such as a ruled grating. By counting the pulses in a given time (an approximation to differentiation) we can estimate velocity, but if we attempt a further differentiation by subtracting successive velocity estimates to obtain acceleration, the result is delayed and prone to disturbance from quantising errors.

Acceleration may be sensed directly by measuring the force on a suspended mass moving with the device under test. Where rapid response is important a convenient sensor is a piezoelectric transducer. This produces charges on opposite faces when it is strained. By using a high input impedance (FET input) amplifier a voltage proportional to charge can be produced, which is thus proportional to the force on the transducer, and then to the acceleration of the suspended mass, and the device to which it is attached.

A device of this kind is called an accelerometer, and one element is sensitive to acceleration in a particular axis.

Multiple sensor devices are available which have two units at right angles, or three at 120° spacing.

The same piezoelectric transducer can be used for pressure measurement but, since the output is a movement of charge and not an e.m.f., the steady-state pressure cannot be determined accurately. However it is convenient for rapidly fluctuating pressures such as are measured in the cylinder of an internal combustion engine.

4.5   Temperature Measurement

All convenient temperature sensors produce analogue outputs. The most precise, and the device generally used as a calibration standard, is the platinum resistance thermometer. This is based upon the experimental relation between resistance and temperature of the form

$$R_t = R_0 \ (1 + At + Bt^2)$$

where

$$R_0 = \text{resistance at } 0\,°C$$
$$R_t = \text{resistance at } t\,°C$$
$$t \ \ = \text{temperature in } °C$$
$$A \ = 3.95 \times 10^{-3}$$
$$B \ = -5.83 \times 10^{-7}$$

The upper limit for this sensor is about 650°C, at which the linear term At exceeds the quadratic term Bt^2 by a factor of 10.4. The non-linearity is thus small over the working range and it can easily be taken into account by a simple calculation once the data have been read into the computer.

Above this temperature, up to about 1700°C, thermocouples can be used. They are generally cheaper and yield a larger signal, and are often used also at lower temperatures.

They comprise a wire circuit consisting of two different materials, with brazed or soldered junctions, and a gap for the measurement of e.m.f. When one junction is heated relative to the other, a small e.m.f. almost proportional to the temperature difference is generated. This varies from about 15 μV per °C to 60 μV per °C depending upon the materials. For low temperatures up to 400°C, copper and constantan are often used, with chrome—nickel and aluminium up to 1300°C and platinum—rhodium and platinum up to 1700°C.

In order to measure absolute temperature it is necessary to maintain the cool junction at a known temperature, or to insert a small voltage which varies with temperature in series with the circuit. This is normally simpler than a thermostat and is called cold junction compensation. A particular advantage of thermo-couples is that fine wire can be used to produce a sensor with a short time constant, of the order of milliseconds.

Several thermocouples can be connected in series to increase the output signal, which is usually connected to an amplifier with a low zero drift, to produce a signal of several volts. This is then suitable for conversion to digital form.

Where precision is less important, greater sensitivity and lower cost can be obtained by using a thermistor. This is a thermally sensitive resistor made from semiconducting metal oxides which is usable up to about 300 °C. Its resistance falls rapidly with temperature, for example from 10 kΩ at 0 °C to about 150 Ω at 100 °C, but in a non-linear manner. These are widely used in domestic equipment such as refrigerators, and washing machines, and in non-critical process controls. Sensitivities vary from 100 mV per °C to 2–5 mV per °C.

Where more accurate readings are necessary a current-generating sensor is now available which, in series with a supply of 5–10 V and a resistor of the order of 10 kΩ, generates a current proportional to absolute temperature. A typical calibration factor is 1 μA per °K. This is much more linear than the thermistor, so no storage of a data table is needed to determine the temperature.

Probably the cheapest temperature sensor is a junction diode. For silicon this has, at constant current, a temperature coefficient for the forward voltage drop of about 2 mV per °C. The difficulty is that there is an additional voltage drop of about 600 mV at 0 °C, so that a 30 °C temperature rise produces a change of only 60 mV in addition to the offset of 600 mV. Despite this, with a stable e.m.f. to balance the offset and an inexpensive operational amplifier a reasonably linear output can be obtained.

All of the above techniques rely on contact between the sensor and the material whose temperature is required. This may not be practicable, and then thermal imaging can be used. This uses a specially corrected lens working with infra-red radiation to produce an image which can be scanned by a radiation detector. Systems of this kind can be used to detect 'hot spots' and so incipient failures in electronic circuits and many types of machinery.

4.6 Signal Conditioning

Typical analogue-to-digital (A/D) signal converters require inputs of 5 V or 10 V, a level much greater than the output of many transducers. Thus some amplification and perhaps zero shifting may be required before a signal can be connected to an A/D converter, a task most conveniently performed by an integrated circuit operational amplifier. This normally has two input terminals, labelled + and −, or 'non-inverting' and 'inverting'. The output voltage V_o is related to the input voltages V_+ and V_- by the expression

$$V_o = A(V_+ - V_- + E_0)$$

Here A is the gain (a positive quantity of the order of 10^4 to 10^5 at low frequencies), V_+ and V_- are the voltages at the + and − inputs respectively, and E_0 is the zero error, or offset at the input.

E_0 is usually of the order of a few millivolts, and most amplifiers have terminals which can be connected to a potentiometer to balance out E_0 where necessary.

The amplifier requires symmetrical power supplies, generally ± 15 V with respect to the signal earth line, and is designed for a full-scale output of just over ± 10 V when supplying a load of 5−10 mA.

The amplifier is usually operated with considerable loop gain, so that to ensure stability the gain is made to fall gradually with frequency until it reaches unity. The frequency at which this occurs may be from 1 MHz, for a cheap high-volume amplifier such as the 741, to 100 MHz for high-frequency devices which can handle a working frequency band of several MHz.

Two basic configurations are widely used for linear amplification, as shown in figure 4.4. Where high input impedance is important, the non-inverting amplifier is preferred; for this circuit a typical inexpensive bipolar amplifier has an input impedance of about 1 MΩ. If this is too small, amplifiers with FET input stages are available which have input impedances of 10^{12} Ω.

Regardless of the characteristics of the amplifier, the input impedance of the inverting amplifier configuration is nearly equal to R_1, normally 1−10 kΩ. If a zero adjustment is required, the circuit of figure 4.2(c) allows an offset to be obtained by adjusting the bias voltage V_2. The output is then

$$V_o = -\frac{R_0}{R_1}(V_1) - \frac{R_0}{R_2}(V_2)$$

If the required relation between V_o and V_1 is $V_o = -a\,V_1 + b$ the resistors and V_2 must satisfy the equations

$$\frac{R_0}{R_1} = a$$

and

$$\frac{R_0}{R_2}(V_2) = -b$$

When a number of analogue inputs are changing relatively slowly, they can

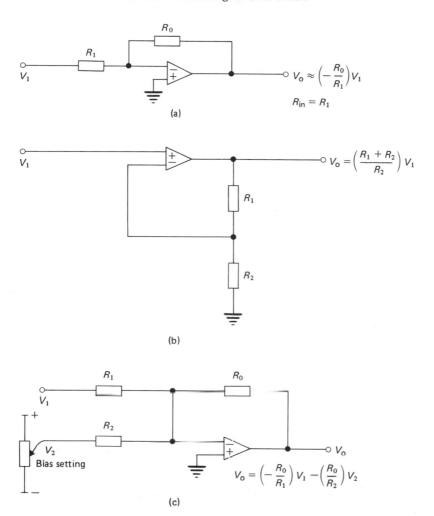

Figure 4.4 Operational amplifier circuits: (a) inverting amplifier;
(b) non-inverting amplifier; (c) inverting amplifier with bias

be sampled sequentially by the same A/D converter by connecting it to each
one in turn. This multiplexing operation can be performed either by reed relays
or for greater speed by FET switches. The process can reduce considerably the
number of relatively expensive A/D converters needed. It can however create a
problem if the various inputs are of differing sizes and so require differing
degrees of amplification to bring them up to a level suitable for A/D conversion.
A single 'switched-gain' amplifier can be used for this by incorporating a range
of resistors in place of R_0, each in series with an FET switch. Thus with R_1 =

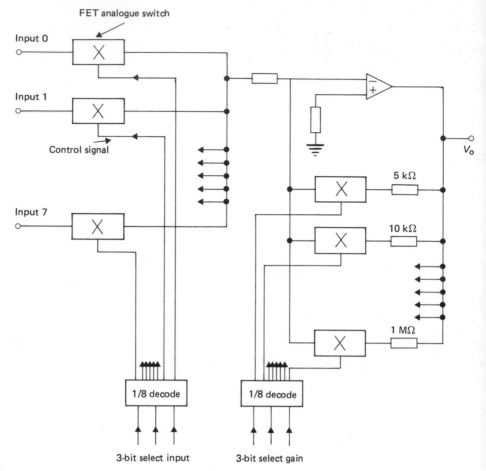

Figure 4.5 Switched gain amplifier and multiplexer

1 kΩ and a range of feedback resistors of 5 kΩ, 10 kΩ, 20 kΩ, 50 kΩ, 100 kΩ, 200 kΩ, 500 kΩ and 1 MΩ, gains of 5, 10, 20, 50, 100, 200, 500 and 1000 are available. In figure 4.5 two 3-to-8-line decoders are used to select one of eight inputs, and one of the above eight gains. This requires six output lines from a peripheral package to control the operation. Three lines select the gain and the other three select which input is sampled.

4.7   Non-linear Operations

All of the previous arrangements discussed for scaling (changing the range of the variable) and shifting the zero have been linear operations. In some situations it may be convenient to introduce some non-linearity, generally to compensate for an opposing non-linearity in the transducer response. This can generally be performed digitally once the signal has reached the processor, but there may not always be time for this. For example, to compute the flow in a pipe containing a venturi constriction the square root of the pressure drop must be evaluated. The basic feedback circuit of figure 4.4(a) can be used to simulate a non-linear response by a piece-wise linear characteristic. The required I/O curve is then approximately generated as ten or so small linear segments by using biased diode or Zener diode branches in parallel with R_1 or R_0. Thus if two Zener diodes back to back are connected in series with a resistor R_2 across the feedback resistor R_0 there will be a breakpoint, or change in slope, at an output voltage equal to the sum of the forward and reverse breakdown voltages of the diodes. Above this voltage, the effective feedback resistor becomes R_0 in parallel with (R_2 + diode slope resistance) and the gain is consequently reduced. More linear segments can be generated by connecting further branches in parallel with R_0.

The result is a sign reversal and a characteristic which is concave upwards. If the characteristic required is concave downwards, the parallel branches must be connected across R_1 rather than R_0.

For some signals having a particularly large dynamic range it may be useful to send to the computer a signal proportional to the logarithm of the input. This can be done by using the exponential relationship between the current in a forward-biased p–n junction and the voltage drop across it. The junction can be the base–emitter junction of a bipolar transistor as shown in figure 4.6. The input signal is taken through a large resistance, so producing an input current I_1 proportional to the input voltage V_i, despite the non-linearity of the junction. The corresponding base–emitter voltage V_{be} contains a variable term proportional to the log of I_1.

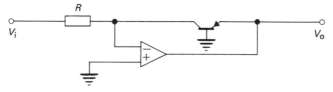

Figure 4.6 Logarithmic amplifier

A frequent requirement is to measure the mean value of an a.c. signal. Passive diode circuits are inaccurate since the silicon diodes generally used do not conduct until the forward bias reaches about 0.5 V. This is 5 per cent of the maximum 10 V signal which most A/D converters can handle. Such an error is usually unacceptable, and active rectifier circuits are used. In these the diodes are connected in the feedback path of an operational amplifier and the high gain substantially masks their imperfections. In the circuit of figure 4.7 we assume a sinusoidal signal input. The input signal is transmitted through resistor R_1 to the second amplifier A_2, and since $R_1 = R_6$, the component of V_0 due to this path is equal to the input V_1 with a sign reversal. The signal at P is negative-going, half-wave rectified, and since $R_6 = 2R_4$, and $R_3 = R_2$, the component of V_0 due to this path is half-wave rectified but doubled in amplitude. There is no sign reversal since there are two amplifiers in cascade. The V_0 signal at the output would thus, in the absence of C, consist of a sinewave from R_1 and a double amplitude positive-going, half-wave rectified sinewave from R_2, R_3, A_1, and R_4. The combined signal is a full-wave rectified signal of amplitude equal to that of the input. Note that the voltage drop across D_2 is in the feedback path and does not contribute to the signal at P.

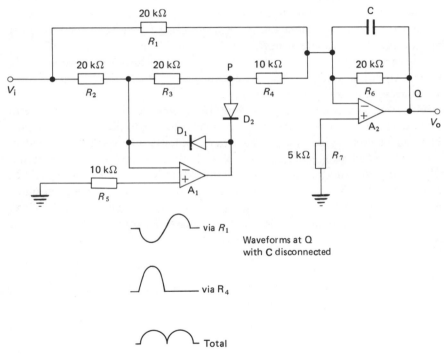

Figure 4.7 Active rectifier circuit

In this circuit zero drift due to temperature changes in amplifier input current is minimised by ensuring that the d.c. resistance from both amplifier inputs to earth is approximately the same, and so the voltage drops due to input current should also be matched. This is the reason for including R_5 and R_7. The arrangement is generally used when low zero drift is important, and the circuit resistance cannot be kept low.

The capacitor C is chosen to provide smoothing of the output voltage, but inevitably it reduces the rate at which V_0 can change.

4.8 Digital to Analogue Converters

Although it could be argued that the logical sequence of material calls for a description of A/D converters first, it is necessary to consider the principles of D/A converters beforehand, since they are generally components of the more complex A/D converters.

Where time is not critical, D/A converters can be made which use time as an intermediate variable. Thus the input number N can be loaded into a counter which is counted down to zero by a pulse train of constant frequency f. The counting period N/f is then proportional to the input number N, and a voltage proportional to this period can be obtained by integrating a reference voltage. This produces an output which changes at a fixed rate, say k V/s. Then if the counting period is T s, the final voltage is $kT = kN/f$, proportional to the original input number N.

An alternative voltage-generating circuit that can be used is the diode pump. This transfers a fixed charge $Q = CV$ from a small capacitor C to a much larger capacitor C_0 for each cycle of the rectangular input waveform. This arrangement thus produces a staircase waveform with the height of each step equal to $Q/C_0 = CV/C_0$ where V is the amplitude of the input waveform.

There are two errors in this expression; a small constant error due to the voltage drop across the diodes, and an increasing error as the voltage on C_0 increases. The latter can be reduced by using the feedback arrangement of figure 4.8. The potential at P hardly changes as it is a virtual earth, so ensuring that each cycle of the input waveform injects the same increment of charge into C_0.

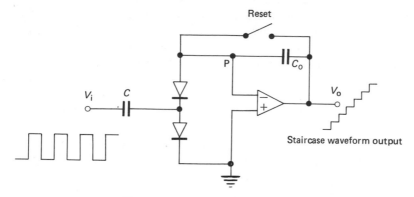

Figure 4.8 Diode pump circuit

The negative-going staircase waveform appears at the output of the amplifier, with almost constant step size.

For some purposes these counting-type converters cause too much delay before the output appears, and parallel converters are required. These are circuits in which the contributions to the output voltage from all bits in the input appear simultaneously, and the only delay is caused by the stray capacitances of the summing network and (usually much larger) the settling time of the summing amplifier. Parallel converters require a set of electronic switches — usually FETs — controlled by the input quantity, connected to a summing amplifier, so that starting from the most significant bit, each successive bit, if 1, contributes exactly half as much as its predecessor. The source of signal is usually a reference potential, and the contributions can be determined either by a series of binary-valued resistors, or by a ladder network having an attenuation of exactly two per stage.

These two methods are shown in figure 4.9. Generally converters handle 8—12 bits, and occasionally more. The graded resistor converter then becomes difficult to make, since there is such a large ratio between the largest resistor and the smallest, and for accuracy these need to have temperature coefficients which are identical to that of the feedback resistor. One way to avoid this problem is to use only a 4-bit network, but to couple this to an identical network through a 16:1 attenuator to give an 8-bit converter; a further attenuator and network produce a 12-bit converter.

The great advantage of the ladder network is that only two resistor values are needed — these can be of the order of $1-2$ kΩ, so having a very low time constant with the stray capacitances. This enables the conversion time to be kept much below $1\,\mu$s if a fast amplifier is used. Times of 50 ns are available from converters developed for high-speed digital systems, such as digital colour television, which use sampling rates around 15 MHz.

For high-accuracy converters the resistor networks are often laser-trimmed, and a high degree of screening is needed to prevent digital signals of several volts causing interference in the analogue output. This can easily occur since the step change for 1-bit in a 5 V 12-bit converter is only 1.25 mV. To minimise the cross-talk there are usually separate analogue and digital earths. It is extremely difficult to avoid some short spikes in the output waveform when the input signal changes. In many situations these are so short that they can be ignored, but when the waveform is used to deflect a CRT for displaying characters or diagrams, the spikes cause momentary movements of the spot and blurr the trace presented.

A solution is to follow the D/A converter output by a sample-and-hold circuit which samples the output a little after a change, when the spike has died away. This circuit in turn feeds the output. A slight delay is introduced, but the resulting signal is much cleaner and so more acceptable. The spikes are often referred to as 'glitches', and the process described above is given the

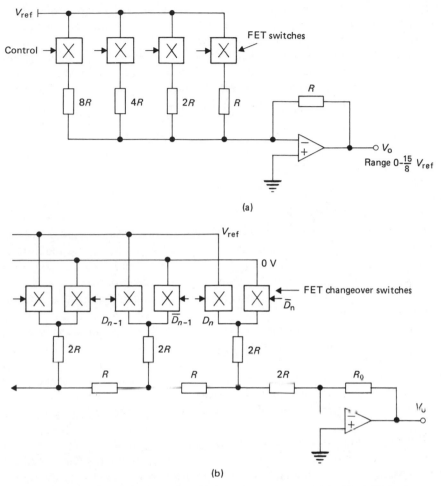

Figure 4.9 Parallel DAC circuits: (a) graded resistor; (b) ladder network

unfortunate name of 'deglitching'.

It is possible to multiplex the output of one D/A converter to several analogues stores, but this is now rarely done as integrated converters have become relatively cheap.

4.9 Analogue to Digital Converters

In general, most A/D converters comprise a D/A converter whose output is compared with the incoming analogue signal by a discriminator or comparator circuit. When the two analogue voltages are equal, the digital input to the DAC is the equivalent of the input. This is essentially an indirect method of conversion and so is slower than D/A conversion.

A simple arrangement is similar to the counter-type DAC; an integrator starts from zero to produce a constant slope or 'ramp' waveform, while a counter counts up from zero. When the integrator output crosses the analogue input voltage, the comparator output changes state and stops the counter. Its contents are then the required digital value. Such a process is slow, and the greater the resolution, the greater the number the counter must handle, and the longer it takes. For example, a 12-bit converter with a clock rate of 20 MHz may take up to about 205 μs to convert.

This is too long for some purposes, and the process can be made much quicker by a trial-and-error procedure. In this the MS bit of a register connected to a DAC is first set to 1, all other bits being zero. The DAC output is then compared to the analogue voltage input. If it exceeds the input, the MS bit is cleared to 0, the next bit is set to 1 and the comparison is repeated. If the DAC output is less than the input, the MS bit is left at 1, and the next bit is also set to 1. The comparison is then repeated. The process continues until all bits have been set and tested. The register then contains the digital equivalent of the input voltage.

This is called the 'successive approximation' A/D converter, and is much faster than the counter ADC. For example the 12-bit converter needs only 12 comparisons to produce the answer instead of up to 4096 using a counter. Even using a slower clock rate, and two periods for the MS bit, the time for a conversion would be reduced to less than 2 μs. This is attainable, but most industrial applications are handled adequately by converters having times of 8–12 μs.

Packaged converters are now available containing all circuits apart perhaps from a clock supply in a single DIL package. If separate units are needed for some particular application, all the logic associated with the setting and clearing of the register is available in an integrated circuit successive approximation register.

Where time is not critical and an inexpensive system is required an A/D converter can be produced with only a D/A converter, a discriminator and an I/O package. The logic of the successive approximation algorithm can then be incorporated in a small program which sets each bit of an output register in turn, and senses the discriminator output through one line of an input port. The output register is embodied in the I/O package by using one port as output which feeds the DAC.

The arrangement is shown in figure 4.10 and the program controlling the action is given below, using a Z80 microprocessor. In this system the program is loaded starting in location 0CE0, and the first 8 bytes set up the control registers of the PIO package. This has port numbers as given below

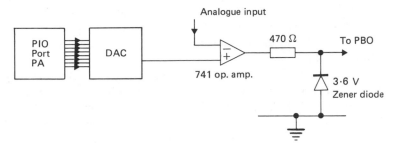

Figure 4.10 ADC circuit for microprocessor

Port no.	Function
04	Data port A
05	Data port B
06	Control port A
07	Control port B

Port A is set for output by sending 0F to its control register, and port B for input by sending 4F to its control register, port 07. These bytes are first assembled in the accumulator using immediate operands. The program uses a pattern of 1000 0000 (80 hexadecimal) which is first loaded into register B. It is sent to the accumulator and output to the DAC to set the MS bit. To allow the operational amplifier and DAC time to settle to a steady output, a delay loop is introduced (locations 0CEE to 0CF2). This takes 128 clock cycles; with a 2 MHz clock supply this requires 64 μs. The system works with an initial count of 04 in location 0CEF, that is, a 32 μs delay, but the count of 08 is used to afford a safety margin.

The amplifier used, a 741, is a low-cost device with a slew rate of only about 0.5 V per μs. Thus a full-scale excursion from −10 V to +10 V will take 40 μs; the signal change at the amplifier output is restricted by the Zener diode so that the time needed to change from about −0.5 V to +4 V will take less than this. However, the amplifier is saturated until the moment when the DAC output and analogue input cross over, and some additional time is needed to return to the linear mode after saturation.

The delay which must be used can be reduced by using a faster DAC and a faster comparator but with extra expense.

After the delay the output of the comparator is read on bit 0 of port B, and if the DAC signal is less than the analogue input the contents of register B are moved one place right, ready to set the next bit along. If the DAC signal is greater than the analogue voltage, the 1 previously sent to the DAC is cancelled by the subtraction instruction in 0CFB. Note that we have used the simple input instruction (op. code DB) which loads the accumulator, so that before this occurs the previous contents of the accumulator, in which the converted value is built up, must be stored. This is done on the stack, and after testing the comparator output the accumulator contents are restored by the POP instructions in 0CFA.

After eight executions of the major loop, the 1 in register B has been shifted out to the right, and it contains zero. This condition terminates the loop and the ADC program. The final action of outputting the converted value to the DAC is not needed generally, but it is convenient for testing when two digital voltmeters are attached to the analogue input and the DAC output, or when one DVM reads the analogue input and a set of binary or hexadecimal displays indicate the digital value sent to the DAC.

As mentioned in the following section, the ADC described above may need to be preceded by a sample-and-hold circuit unless the slew rate is very low. This is due to the rather long conversion time required by the program.

Program 4.1   ADC Program Using Successive Approximation Algorithm

Location	Instruction		Code	Comment
CE0		LDA, # 0F	3E	Set up pattern in AC for
1			0F	port A as output
2		OUT 07	D3	Send to port A
3			07	control register
4		LDA, # 4F	3E	Set up pattern in AC for
5			4F	port B as input
6		OUT 06	D3	Send to port B
7			06	control register
8		LDB, # 80	06	Set MSB in register B
9			80	
A		SUBA, A	97	Clear AC
B	START:	ADDA, B	80	Enter, MS bit
C		OUT 05	D3	Output to DAC
D			05	
E	LOOP:	LD D # 08	16	Enter delay loop
F			08	in register D
CF0		DEC D	15	Decrement D
1		JRNZ LOOP	20	Repeat if not zero
2			FD	
3		PUSH AF	F5	Store AC contents
4		IN 04	DB	Read discriminator
5			04	output
6		CMP # 00	FE	Compare with zero
7			00	
8		JRNZ TOOLO	28	Jump if DAC output
9			04	is less than input

A	TOOHI:	POP AF	F1	Fetch AC contents
B		SUB A, B	98	Clear current bit
C		JR SHIFT	18	Jump to SHIFT
D			01	
E	TOOLO:	POP AF	F1	Fetch AC contents
F	SHIFT:	SH RT B LOG	CB	Shift mask right one place
DO0			38	
1		JR NZ START	20	Repeat if all 8 bits
2			E8	have not been tested
3		OUT 05	D3	Output final
4			05	value
5		CALL MON	C3	Return to
6			59	system
7			03	monitor

4.10 Slew Rate Limitations

Successive approximation A/D converters are widely used on account of their characteristics of fast conversion and moderate cost, which enable them to meet many applications for data conversion. However, they have one particular disadvantage in that, to ensure minimum error, the input signal must change by less than the equivalent of 1 LS bit during the conversion time. This is because the process is a sequential one, with no opportunity for changing decisions once made. For example, if the input signal begins to change after the first two digits have been set at 00, the change may be sufficient to reach a value corresponding to the digits 01. Since each bit is tested only once, there is no opportunity for changing the second bit subsequently and the final result will be in error.

This restriction can in a high-resolution converter limit the permissible bandwidth very severely.

If we consider a 12-bit ADC with a nominal range of 0–10 V, the LS bit is equivalent to a voltage change of

$$\frac{10 \text{ V}}{4096} = 2.44 \text{ mV}$$

For a conversion time of 15 μs, the maximum slew rate for a change not exceeding 1 LS bit in this period is

$$\frac{dV}{dt} = \frac{2.44 \times 10^{-3}}{15 \times 10^{-6}} \quad \text{V/s}$$

$$= 162.7 \text{ V/s}$$

The largest sine wave which can be correctly measured can then be calculated since a signal $v = V \sin \omega t$ has a slew rate of $dv/dt = \omega V \cos \omega t$, whose maximum value is ωV V/s. Now with a peak-to-peak (p–p) range of 10 V the amplitude of a sine wave cannot exceed 5 V and thus the limiting condition is given by

$$\omega \times 5 = \frac{dV}{dt}_{max} = 162.7 \text{ V/s}$$

whence $\omega = 32.53$ radians/s

and $f = 5.178$ Hz

This is a very small upper frequency and quite unacceptable for many applications. The way to avoid this limitation is to take a sample of the signal prior to conversion and to hold this sample constant during conversion. There is still some error, because when the sampling pulse is generated the action begins on the leading edge of the pulse. The circuit must first change the output so that it becomes equal to the input – the 'acquisition' phase. It then tracks the changing input and, when the sampling pulse ends, the output is held constant until the next sampling pulse arrives. The error arises because the value held and then converted to digital form is that corresponding to the end of the sampling pulse, whereas the value expected is that at the beginning of the sampling pulse.

The error is minimised by using very short sampling pulses. For example, in the above case a sampling pulse of 20 ns would permit a slew rate of

$$\frac{2.44 \times 10^{-3}}{20 \times 10^{-9}} \quad \text{V/s}$$

$$= \frac{2\,440\,000}{20} \quad = 122\,000 \text{ V/s}$$

whence the maximum frequency of the same 5 V sine wave is given by

$$5\omega = 122\,000 \text{ V/s}$$
$$\text{whence } f = \frac{122\,000}{10\pi}$$
$$= 3.88 \text{ kHz}$$

This is still quite a small bandwidth, and for wideband signals such as colour television, an 8-bit converter needs a sampling period of only a few hundred picoseconds (10^{-12} s).

The circuit concerned is called a 'sample-and-hold' circuit and involves high-current drive amplifiers and storage in a capacitor. A typical circuit is shown in figure 4.11.

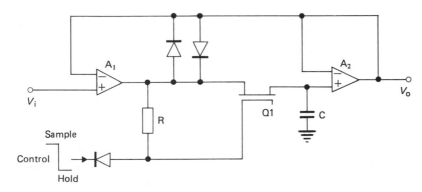

Figure 4.11 Sample-and-hold circuits

Amplifier A_1 needs to provide a high output to charge the storage capacitor C quickly during the sample period. Amplifier A_2 needs a high input impedance to minimise the degree to which C is discharged during the hold period. Overall feedback is included to diminish the error during the sampling period. The two diodes are provided to give some degree of feedback for A_1 during the hold period when the FET is open circuit. Without these A_1 would saturate under open-loop conditions and would introduce a delay on account of the extra time needed to recover. In some designs the diodes are replaced by another FET which is fed with an inverted control signal, so that it conducts only when Q1 is open circuit.

In figure 4.11 Q1 is an *n*-channel FET, so that a negative control signal biases it off, and a positive signal allows the resistor R to return the gate to the channel potential, so giving full conduction. In fast circuits a limit to the charging rate is imposed by the FET on-resistance. In the circuit shown this quantity is inside the feedback loop and so its effect is much reduced. The dominant limit to the slew rate of the capacitor voltage is the current available from A_1. For example, if the acquisition time must not exceed 20 ns and the change in voltage since the last sample may be 5 V, if $C = 500$ pF the mean charging current is

$$I = \frac{CV}{t} = \frac{500 \times 10^{-12} \times 5}{20 \times 10^{-9}} \text{ A}$$

$$= 125 \text{ mA}$$

Sample-and-hold units are now available in integrated form, in which the only external component needed is a low-leakage (plastic film) storage capacitor. They are usually incorporated in packaged high-accuracy A/D converters.

4.11   Tracking Converters

One way to avoid the need for a sample-and-hold circuit is to reduce the conversion time to something less than an instruction time. This can be done by using a tracking ADC in which a DAC is connected to the output of a counter and the counter is controlled by a comparator output. It differs from the counter-type ADC in that the comparator does not stop the clock supply when the DAC output exceeds the analogue input: it reverses the direction of counting. The clock supply is continuous, so that as the analogue voltage changes, the ADC output and so the counter contents follow or 'track' it. When the analogue input remains steady, the digital output hunts up and down by a count of one.

There is a limit to the rate of tracking; for an N-bit counter full-scale corresponds to 2^N bits and so one bit corresponds to a voltage increment of $V/2^N$ and with a clock frequency of f Hz takes a time $1/f$ s. The slew rate is thus $Vf/2^N$ and, should the analogue input change more rapidly than this, the DAC will be unable to keep up with it and a serious error may occur.

For example, a 10-bit system with a 5-volt range and a counting rate of 10 MHz (within the capacity of standard TTL) has a maximum slew rate of

$$\frac{Vf}{2^N} = \frac{5 \times 10^7}{1024} = 48\,830 \text{ V/s}$$

whence the maximum frequency of a 5 V p—p sine wave which could be tracked correctly is given by equating this slew rate to the peak slew rate of the sine wave.

Thus $2.5 \times \omega = 48\,830$ V/s
or $f = 3.11$ kHz

This type of ADC has severe slew rate limitations if high resolution is required, but it has major operational advantages over slower ADCs in that it needs a minimum of interface hardware and program. The counter contents can be read by the computer at any time, and there is no conversion delay. The only condition is that the counter contents should not be changing when the processor reads them. This can be avoided by using the processor clock, or a signal derived from it, as the counter clock, so synchronising the counter changes to the processor clock.

The only hardware needed is one or more input ports to read the counter contents, and the only program one or more instructions to perform the input transfer.

In contrast the successive approximation ADC needs an extra control line to start the conversion cycle and a sense line to determine when the conversion is finished and the data are ready for input.

The program must issue the start command, test whether the output is ready and if not repeat the test. Only when the test is successful can the data be read into the processor.

4.12 Digital Coding of Analogue Signals

Where an analogue signal is of only one polarity, coding is simple. The digital value is linearly related to the analogue input so that for example, in an 8-bit converter 0000 0000 or 00 (hexadecimal) corresponds to 0 V, and the MS bit 1000 0000 or 80 (hexadecimal) corresponds to half full-scale (5 V in a 10-volt converter). The maximum output occurs when the digital signal has its maximum value of FF, which produces 10 V × 255/256 = 9.961 V.

To produce bipolar signals, say in the range ±10 V, a DAC coded as above can be followed by an amplifier with a zero offset of – 10 V and a gain of 2. Then an input 00 will produce the offset output of – 10 V; the MSB alone, 80, will produce 0 V, and the greatest positive value is generated by FF, and is now 10 V × 127/128 = 9.922 V.

This coding is simple to obtain from a unipolar DAC (the easiest type to make) but it is not used inside the processor, where numbers are usually handled in 2's complement form. The 2's complement form can be obtained simply by inverting the MS bit of the offset code, so that an input of 00 produces an output of 0 V. The most negative output of – 10 V is generated by the digital input 80, and the most positive voltage of 9.922 V by 7F. The input FF now produces the smallest negative signal of – 10 V/128 = – 78.13 mV, corresponding to a digital value of – 1 LS bit.

Most A/D and D/A converters operate only on unipolar signals, but some of the more complex packages provide alternative feedback resistors and arrangements for an optional offset so that by suitable connections unipolar, offset bipolar or 2's complement coding can be handled.

4.13 ADC Interfacing

The extra complication which arises when using a counter-type or successive approximation ADC is caused by the time lag between starting conversion and the data becoming available.

Thus if we use two successive instructions such as

(1) send output pulse to start ADC

(2) read data from ADC output register

the result will be grossly in error unless we have a very fast ADC. The time taken to execute the second instruction is likely to be only 3–5 μs, considerably less than the 12–30 μs or more which a typical ADC requires to complete a conversion. Thus the above program tries to read the data long before they are ready.

One way to avoid this error is to interpose a delay loop between the two instructions to give the ADC time to complete its conversion. The duration of the delay loop should be somewhat greater than the conversion time, and it is usually provided by loading a value into one of the accumulators and decrementing it down to zero. However, the conversion time, particularly with a counter-type ADC, depends upon the analogue input, and the average delay could be reduced if the data could be read as soon as they became available, instead of having a fixed delay decided by the longest possible conversion time. This needs a signal from the ADC to the processor in addition to the signal in the reverse direction to start conversion. Many ADCs provide a 'busy' signal which is normally at logic 0 and changes to logic 1 during conversion, reverting to 0 when conversion has finished.

To illustrate the process we take as an example an 8-bit ADC interfaced through a PIA to an M6800, using port A for the data input. Control line CA1 can be used to sense the state of the busy line, by setting flag 1 on the negative-going (1 $\rightarrow$ 0) transition, and CA2 can be programmed to give a short positive pulse to start conversion.

The program must first set up the control register, then start the ADC, wait in a loop continually testing flag 1, and leave the loop when the flag is set. The final action is to read the data into the processor.

Assuming that the system has just been reset when power was applied, all PIA registers are cleared, and PA will be set for input. The control register CRA must then be programmed as follows

CA1 – no interrupts; must sense the busy signal and set flag 1 on a 1 $\rightarrow$ 0 transition.

CA2 – set for output, to provide a start conversion signal; here programmed to follow the data output to bit 3 of CRA.

Bit CRA2 must be set to allow future access to PA for reading the ADC output. If bits CRA4 and CRA5 are both 1, values written to CRA3 will be copied out on CA2 to produce a 'start conversion' pulse. Bits CRA6 and CRA7 are read only and the write action has no effect. Here we put zeros into CRA6 and CRA7. The complete control byte for CRA is thus, 0011 1100 or 3C (hexadecimal). This must be followed immediately by 0011 0100 or 34 to end the 'start conversion' pulse. No input to DDRA is needed since the initial reset will clear it to zero, so setting PA for 8 input lines.

The program must then read the control register and sense the flag CRA7 which will be set as soon as conversion finishes. Meanwhile the program waits in a loop. In the following program segment we omit any action on port B or control register CRB as these are not needed. In general however, DDRB and CRB would be set up in the same initialising process, and there may well be other activity such as initialising the stack pointer, or other peripheral packages intervening between the initialising and the beginning of the ADC operation.

Program for Controlling ADC Coupled to M6800

Instruction	Code	Comment
LDA A #3C	86	Load bit pattern for CRA
	3C	
STA A 4001	B7	Load CRA, generate 'start
	40	conversion' pulse
	01	
LDA A #34	86	Load same bit pattern, but with
	34	bit 3 = 0
STA A 4001	B7	Clear CRA3, so ending 'start
	40	conversion' pulse
	01	
LOOP: LDA A 4001	B6 ←	Read control register CRA
	40	
	01	
BPL LOOP	2A	Repeat if bit 7 is clear
	FB	
LDA A 4000	B6	Read ADC output
	40	
	00	Rest of program
	—	
	—	
	—	

The register addresses for port A of the PIA are

$$4000 - \text{PA and DDRA}$$
$$4001 - \text{CRA}$$

The above program ends with the data in accumulator A. Where a series of measurements are being taken, there may not be sufficient time between readings for the computation required and the program may then merely load the readings into a block of writable store, and when the block has been filled divert control to another program which analyses the data.

Where the readings are taken under the control of external timing pulses, the same procedure can be used, with another flag and waiting loop arranged to hold the processor until the next pulse appears. However, if the pulses are irregular in timing or well spaced, much more computation can be performed if the external pulses create an interrupt and invoke the conversion routine. The processor can then spend the rest of the time on other useful calculations. A slightly more efficient procedure is to connect the external pulse to the start conversion input to the ADC. The end of the busy signal must then be used to cause an interrupt. By this means the processor can continue calculation while conversion takes place, only being interrupted when the data are ready.

4.14 Other Types of A/D Converter

Apart from the tracking ADC other converters described previously are all sequential in operation. Where very high speed is essential, parallel operation is called for, but these require much more hardware. A completely parallel or 'flash' encoder needs one comparator for each voltage level. This is an attainable goal with modern microelectronic techniques. For example a single chip containing a precision resistor chain and 16 comparators can be produced using very fast ECL circuits; 16 of these with some extra logic produce an 8-bit ADC with a sampling rate of 100 MHz.

The advent of MOS technology enables very high input impedance amplifiers to be constructed, and a very compact version of the graded resistor DAC shown in figure 4.9(a) can be produced by replacing the resistors with capacitors. Since capacitors are easier to fabricate accurately, and need a smaller area of silicon than resistors, this version is more suitable for integration. It is often called a 'charge balance' DAC.

4.15   Protection from Interference

An essential feature of microprocessors, built as they are on a single chip of silicon, is that the capacitance of each active element is low, and the signal level is only a few volts. Thus the charge needed to switch a circuit may be no more than tens of picocoulombs. If we consider using this equipment to control a petrol engine, the ignition leads will have voltage transients of typically 20 kV when the engine is cold. For a bistable needing a 3 V trigger signal and having an input capacitance of 8 pF the charge needed to switch is 24 pC. This will be induced into the bistable if the capacitance between the microprocessor circuit and the ignition lead is 0.0012 pF or more.

Clearly in this kind of environment extraordinarily effective screening of all the microelectronic circuits is required. This can be ensured by using a continuous metal enclosure for the microprocessor and its associated circuits, but this of course requires external connections for power supplies and signal I/O. Every external lead is a potential source of interference and may need preventive treatment.

The first consideration is the power supply. In order to provide a constant potential regardless of fluctuations in the primary mains or battery supply, high-gain regulators are generally used to supply the microprocessor and peripheral logic. Regulators of adequate current handling capacity (3 A at 5 V) are now available in integrated circuit form, but owing to their high gain these frequently generate high-frequency oscillations which can be reduced to acceptable proportions only by adequate decoupling capacitors wired directly to the package. Failure to observe the recommended precautions can cause errors in the circuits supplied.

A major failure mode of these and discrete component regulators is a short-circuit in the series pass transistor, thus connecting the raw d.c. supply directly to the load. This is usually high enough to cause irreparable damage to the microprocessor and other circuits, and is often caused by high-voltage transients fed along the supply lines.

There are two methods of combating this problem. The first is to filter carefully all incoming supplies to reduce the likelihood of a damaging transient. Secondly, if some major failure should generate a transient large enough to disturb the regulated supply, a 'crowbar' circuit can be added. This is a circuit which effectively short-circuits the power supply if the voltage becomes excessive (say 6.5 V on a nominal 5 V supply), so causing a fuse to blow. For low current circuits up to a rated current of perhaps 0.5 A a power Zener diode will suffice; above this a thyristor is generally used with a small limiting resistor in series. The resistor in this case protects the thyristor by limiting the short-circuit current. The thyristor circuit often has the gate fed from a potentiometer which is in series with a Zener diode across the supply. This enables the critical voltage to be adjusted accurately.

Power supplies also need good HF decoupling against transients caused by rapidly changing logic loads. These are most effective when placed as close as possible to the logic circuits. TTL packages are the worst sources of noise on the supply line and may require a small ceramic decoupling capacitor, say 5 nF for each four packages.

MOS logic, as used in most microprocessors, switches more slowly and needs less decoupling. One source of power supply noise is mains-borne interference. This can be reduced by filtering the incoming mains supply and by using a mains transformer with an earthed electrostatic shield between primary and secondary.

The other source of interference arises from conduction along the signal input and output lines. Looking first at the input lines, the obvious initial step is to filter all of them so that only signals within the working bandwidth are permitted access. The reason for this is that both impulsive noise and random noise are signals with energy distributed over a wide bandwidth, and reducing the bandwidth will reduce the total noise voltage. Fortunately many inputs from manual controls, keyboards and switches of various kinds because of their inertia are not capable of changing state very rapidly, and so drastic lowpass filtering can be used. Where the interference is at a particular frequency, for example mains frequency, narrow-band rejection circuits can be used, or for signals with a small slew rate, integrating A/D converters can be used with the conversion time adjusted to one cycle of the mains. This substantially cancels out the single-frequency interference. Where some random noise remains after filtering it may be possible to take a number of samples and average them, so increasing the signal-to-noise ratio.

A particularly difficult source of interference is common-mode noise. This arises when both lines of an incoming circuit have voltages induced in them which, with respect to earth, may be much larger than the differential signal between the lines which is to be measured. Special amplifiers are available with high differential gain and very low common-mode gain, but these are expensive and can deal with only limited common-mode voltages.

For digital signals, nearly complete isolation of common-mode voltages can be obtained quite cheaply by using optical isolators. These consist of a photo-transistor and a light-emitting diode encased in transparent plastic, in an opaque enclosure. The two components are close enough to give good optical coupling, but typically provide electrical isolation that will withstand 2.5 kV. The capacitance between input and output is of the order of 1 pF, which is not sufficient to permit any significant transmission of the noise. These devices are not particularly linear, but with some degree of compensation they have been used for isolating analogue signals where extreme linearity is not required. Fully isolating amplifiers are available in which the analogue signal modulates a carrier, allowing transformer coupling to be used for isolation, but these are expensive. Much protection against capacitively coupled noise can be obtained by using screened cable, in the worst cases with double screens, but inductively coupled noise can be reduced only by using tightly twisted pairs and choosing the route carefully.

The recent development of optical fibre links has reduced their price so that they become an attractive proposition for electrically noisy environments. They are quite impervious to all types of electrical interference and their only disadvantage is the need to multiplex all data along a single serial channel. They offer, for example, much the most economical way to transmit computer input and output to the beam control circuits of a particle accelerator which may be working at potentials of several hundred kilovolts above earth.

Low-level analogue signals are inherently much more prone to suffer from induced noise than digital signals which usually have amplitudes of several volts. Thus the effect of noise can be much reduced by transforming analogue signals into digital form as near to the source as possible, and transmitting them at fairly high level along balanced circuits. Special integrated circuits are available which drive the lines differentially with current of 12 mA and their corresponding receivers can reliably sense 25 mV of differential signal masked by up to ± 3 V of common-mode noise.

In addition to input lines, output lines feeding high-power devices such as triacs, thyristors and high-power transistors need some isolation to prevent transients from them reaching the microprocessor circuits.

4.16 Output Circuits

For many applications power gain and circuit isolation can both be provided by driving relays or contactors from the computer outputs. The main requirement is for some current gain to provide adequate driving power. Small relays can be driven directly from a single transistor as shown in figure 4.12, with a protection diode to prevent overvoltage transients when the transistor current is turned off. Where continuous operation occurs under adverse electrical conditions a 'solid-state relay' may be used. This is a thyristor or power transistor which can switch a substantial load, isolated from the microprocessor circuits by an optical isolator.

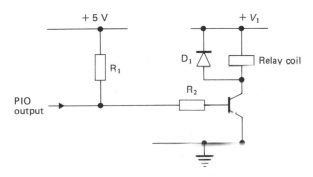

Figure 4.12 Relay driving circuit

In addition to switching currents on or off there may be a requirement for a varying current or voltage. For moderate powers of tens of watts this can be provided by a D/A converter feeding a linear power amplifier, but for higher powers a much more economical process is to use a switched mode of operation in which the amplifier is supplied with a pulse of constant frequency and varying mark-to-space ratio. A crude 8-level arrangement can be provided very simply by connecting an 8-bit shift register to an 8-bit output port. The shift register is connected to recirculate its data, and is loaded in parallel with a byte of data. The power amplifier is fed from the recirculated data and its mean output level is proportional to the number of 1's in the output byte. Where more precise control is needed a counter/timer package can be used in which one counter generates the mark period and another the space period. Using 8-bit counters provides sufficient resolution for many purposes, but greater resolution can be obtained if the full 16-bit count is used.

A similar timing problem occurs when using thyristors or triacs to control a.c. supplies. Here the timing pulse must be delayed by a controlled amount to adjust the mean current flowing. A counter/timer can be used conveniently to produce the time delay, but this must be measured from the instant when the mains voltage crosses zero. For this purpose special integrated circuits are available which generate a pulse at each crossing; this must be sensed by the microprocessor and used to start the counting interval. Generally a current of 30—40 mA at a voltage of 2.5—3 V will trigger the thyristor or triac, and allowing some margin above this the pulse can easily be generated by a single transistor. It is customary to use an isolating transformer to couple the transistor collector to the solid-state switch and, as with a relay, a protective diode is needed across the transformer primary. Some form of current limiting is often provided to safeguard the driving transistor.

4.17   Motor Drive Circuits

Large d.c. motors are generally supplied by triacs or thyristors. Thyristors can be used in a full wave bridge circuit, and for economical operation only two of the four rectifying elements need the thyristors, the others being diodes as shown in figure 4.13. This drive will operate only in one direction; if it is necessary to reverse the motor a contactor can be used to interchange the motor terminals, or a bridge circuit comprising four thyristors can be used in conjunction with a rectified supply as shown in figure 4.14. Here thyristors A and D are energised for forward rotation, B and C for reverse.

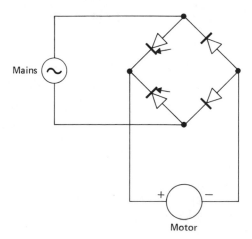

Figure 4.13 Half bridge thyristor motor drive circuit

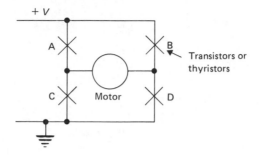

Figure 4.14 Reversing motor drive circuit

A similar circuit can be used for low-power motors requiring some tens of watts by replacing the thyristors by power transistors.

For high-power applications three-phase rectification would normally be used, as this provides a balanced load on the supply.

5 Single - chip Microprocessors

5.1 Applications of Single-chip Systems

Some years after the introduction of the second generation of 8-bit microprocessors, the rapidly expanding market revealed a wealth of applications
which required only modest provision of program and data storage and I/O
lines. Many of these were in domestic equipment and simple machinery such
as petrol pumps. Improvements in manufacturing techniques enabled an 8-bit
processor, 1K bytes of ROM and 64 bytes of RAM, together with 20 or more
I/O lines to be fabricated on a single chip. The result is a single package which
needs only a clock supply and a reset signal to produce a complete microprocessor system.

The clock-maintaining circuits are built on the chip, so only a crystal
resonator or a small inductor, together with two small capacitors, are required
externally. The reset pin needs to be held below the logic 0 threshold for a
few milliseconds after power has been applied – a C–R circuit will suffice for
this.

Where such a device can be used the microprocessor hardware is much
cheaper and more compact than that of earlier systems which required separate
packages for CPU, ROM, RAM and I/O, and all the attendant wiring.

5.2 Typical One-chip Devices – the Intel 8048 Family

One of the early groups of single-chip microprocessors was based upon the
Intel 8048. This device is intended for high-volume applications where at least
some thousands of identical devices are needed. The program store is mask-
programmed by the maker during fabrication. For lower-volume products
a user-programmable version, the 8748, is available. This has a UV-erasable
program store of 1K bytes, and is pin-compatible with the 8048. Both versions
have 64 bytes of RAM, 27 I/O lines and an 8-bit interval timer/event counter.
The erasable store makes it also very convenient for development. Where extra
storage is needed, another version, the 8035, is available which has no internal
program store. This enables the user to attach any convenient form of program
storage to the CPU package.

All of these devices require only a single 5 V supply. The I/O lines comprise
two 8-bit ports, and an 8-bit data bus which also carries the 8 low-order bits of
the program counter during an instruction fetch from external program store.

The processor can conveniently be used with 8085 peripheral devices since an address latch pulse ALE is provided to enable the address information to be stored pending the arrival of a data byte. Two test inputs T0 and T1 are provided, with branch instructions which operate when the inputs are high (JT0, JT1) or low (JNT0, JNT1).

A single interrupt line is available which can be enabled or disabled by program.

The architecture differs in several respects from that of the 8080 and 8085 processors. There is no stack pointer register, but a stack can be operated in the 64 bytes of RAM provided on the chip. Eight general-purpose registers are available, of which R0 and R1 can be used as pointers to one of the bytes of the RAM.

The instruction set is chosen to be convenient for control applications rather than arithmetic; for example there is no subtract instruction, neither is there an arithmetic shift. Any bit of internal or external data can however be tested by moving the byte concerned into the accumulator and using the 'jump on accumulator bit' instruction. This causes a jump if the bit specified is set. The majority of instructions occupy 1 byte; only branches and instructions with immediate operands need 2 bytes.

In order to assist in handling interrupts quickly, a duplicate set of 8 CPU registers is provided in the RAM area (bank 1). These can be selected by a single byte instruction, and another similar instruction will return control to the former bank 0 registers when the interrupt has been serviced.

1K bytes of on-chip program storage are provided, and a further 1K bytes can be added and addressed by the same instructions.

If more program space is needed, the 'select memory bank 1' instruction changes control to the program store in locations 2048_{10} to 4095_{10}.

An interesting feature is that the same address space can be used by both program and data storage, so economising on the number of address pins needed. The program store is selected by a processor output signal 'program store enable' which is issued when an instruction is fetched, but not for a data address.

Either R0 or R1 may be used to address up to 256 bytes of external data store.

Where the two ports cannot provide sufficient I/O lines, a further 16 can be added by attaching an 8243 expander. This has four data input pins, normally driven by half a processor port, and one of the remaining lines of the port is used as a chip select signal. The PROG pin used to program the 8748 store also serves as an output strobe for the expander.

This arrangement can be extended to three further expander packages by using the last three lines of port 2 (P25, P26 and P27) as chip select signals in the same manner as P24 is used to select the first 8243 package.

The external lines of the 8243 are grouped into four sets of four, multiplexed to P20–P23 which are connected to pins P20–P23 of the processor as shown in figure 5.1. All data transfers involve two 4-bit nibbles sent to P20–P23. The first specifies the port (4, 5, 6 or 7) and the operation (read, write, OR, AND). The second consists of the data. All transfers are to or from the accumulator. The two logical operations can be performed on the existing contents of the output register only in a write operation.

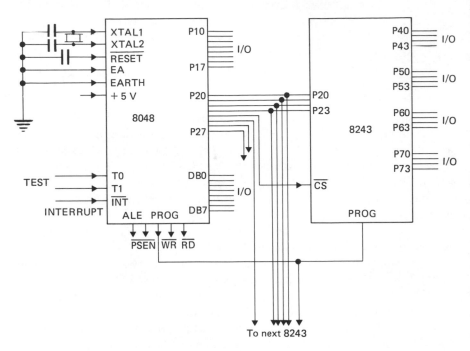

Figure 5.1 Using 8243 I/O Expander with Intel 8048

In order to reduce the need for extra current amplifiers the output drive capacity of the 8243 has been made greater than many earlier MOS packages. Each of the 16 output lines can sink 5 mA, but if some of them are not required to carry this current, the remaining lines can handle greater current. The lines of port 7 in particular can carry up to 20 mA, but if they were all loaded fully no other port could be used for output.

Figure 5.1 also illustrates an important feature of single-chip microprocessors, that is, the relatively small number of components needed to assemble a working system.

Other expansion facilities are provided by the 8155 (256 bytes of RAM, two 8-bit ports, one 6-bit port and a programmable 14-bit timer/counter) and the 8355 and 8755A program stores. The 8355 is mask-programmed and provides 2K bytes of program storage and two 8-bit ports, each line of which can be individually programmed input or output. The 8755A is pin-compatible and performs the same function, but it has a user-programmable, UV-erasable store.

Many of the applications of single-chip microprocessors are to domestic or industrial products which accept data from, or output data to, a human operator or user. Generally input is via a keyboard, or touch panel, and output via numerical displays. So many microprocessors need this type of input or output that manufacturers provide special interface packages for scanning a keyboard and driving an alphanumeric display or a bank of indicator lamps.

These packages simplify the design of the microprocessor system and reduce the program space considerably as they perform the scanning of the keyboard by hardware rather than software. Also by using a 40-pin package sufficient output lines are available to multiplex a 16-character display, refreshed from the package rather than from the processor. The burden on the processor is thus much reduced, since it is not required to scan the keys or refresh the display continually. The only connections to the processor needed by a typical programmable keyboard/display interface package, the Intel 8279, are

Data bus	D0–D7
Interrupt line	INT
Read strobe	$\overline{RD}$
Write strobe	$\overline{WR}$
Chip select	$\overline{CS}$
Reset	$\overline{RESET}$
Clock	CLK
Register select	C/D

The last signal is normally connected to address line A0; A0 = 1 denotes a command or status byte, A0 = 0 denotes a data byte. When $\overline{CS}$ is logic 1 the chip is not selected and the data bus drivers are high impedance. The clock pin is normally driven by the system clock and it supplies the internal timing signals through a built-in prescaler. This has a command byte of the form 001 DDDDD where the five LS bits determine the division ratio. This should be set to produce an internal clock of about 100 kHz, to ensure that the 'debounce' and scan times generated are of the correct length.

The keyboard scanning signals can handle up to 64 keys, and generate a 6-bit code which indicates the position of the key depressed. If needed, an interrupt can be signalled at the same time. The display lines provide 8-segment lines and four scan counter lines which can select one of 16 display devices.

In order to handle this combination of input and output the 8279 requires in addition to the keyboard and multiplexed display devices, a 3-to-8 decoder to select one of 8 rows of the keyboard matrix and a 4-to-16 decoder to select one of the 16 character displays.

5.3   The Intel 8021 and 8022

The Intel 8021 and 8022 were designed as part of the 8048 family for low-cost, high-volume applications requiring limited data and program storage space. They include only 64 bytes of data storage, and 1K (8021) or 2K (8022) bytes of program storage, with no facilities for additional external storage. This means that the data bus need not be extended outside the processor chip, so saving pins.

The 8021 uses only 30 pins and provides three 8-bit ports; the 8022 uses the conventional 40-pin package and in addition to the three 8-bit ports it provides for two analogue input signals, either of which can be switched to an 8-bit A/D converter on the chip. To reduce digital cross-talk in the analogue circuits separate 5 V and reference supply pins are used.

Both the 8021 and 8022 have 8-bit timers/event counters and have one input which allows zero-crossing sensing of a small voltage of mains frequency. They incorporate mask ROM, but for development the manufacturer supplies a small emulation board which contains a special 8021 or 8022 which reads its program from a UV-erasable 8748 EPROM package.

Where more I/O lines are needed the 8243 expander package can be added to both processors.

The zero-crossing detector and the timer enable the processors to generate pulses having any required phase delay with respect to the zero-crossing instant of a 50 Hz mains supply. These features are particularly convenient for controlling power supplied to d.c. and a.c. loads, for applications such as heating control, motor controls, etc. The analogue inputs of the 8022 can be used for temperature measurement, so enabling it to be used for closed-loop control of heating systems, cookers and microwave ovens.

5.4   The Zilog Z8 Family

This family of single-chip microprocessors is aimed at somewhat more complex applications than those for which the earlier Intel range was intended. The Z8601 has 2K bytes of mask-programmed ROM, 128 bytes of RAM, 32 I/O lines, and can be extended to handle up to 62K bytes of both program and data storage. It has a full duplex UART for serial data, and two programmable 8-bit counter/timers. When the UART is used, one of the counters supplies the bit rate signal. An 8-bit stack pointer is available for the on-chip RAM, but this extends to 16 bits when the stack resides in external RAM. The 8-bit ports are arranged to have different functions to allow for the widest range of applications. Port 0 is divided into two 4-bit sections, each of which can be programmed as inputs or outputs. When external storage is used, the lines can be programmed to supply address lines A8–A11 or A8–A15. Port 1 can be programmed as a byte input or byte output port, or as an address/data port when using external storage, to access locations above 2048_{10}.

Port 2 can have its lines programmed independently as inputs or outputs, like the M6820 PIA ports. Port 3 always provides four inputs and four outputs. These can be used for I/O transfers, or as control lines.

In the latter mode they provide handshaking signals for ports 0, 1 and 2 (ready, and data available), four external interrupt request signals, timer input and output signals, and a data memory select signal. The interrupts have a built-in priority order, and are individually maskable. Their vector addresses are held in locations $0-11_{10}$ of the program store, and after reset the program begins in the following location, and can occupy the remaining 2036_{10} bytes of the on-chip ROM.

The requirement for building prototype systems for the testing and development of both hardware and software is satisfied in a different manner from that used for the 8048 family. The change is largely a consequence of the different pin assignments, and encompasses two packages, the Z8602 and the Z8603.

The Z8602 enables all software to be tested using a processor which is program compatible with that of the Z8601, but with the following electrical changes

(a) it is mounted in a 64-pin package
(b) it has no internal program store
(c) the data, address and control lines of the program store are buffered and brought out to external pins, so enabling the program to be held in any convenient EPROM or RAM.

The Z8602 enables the hardware to be checked, but not in its final production form as it is not pin-compatible with the mask-programmed Z8601. In order to achieve this final check the Z8603 has been produced. This is a standard Z8601 with the ROM omitted, but with the ROM lines connected to a 'piggy-back' socket. This is a 24-pin DIL socket mounted on the upper surface of the Z8603 into which a 2716 EPROM can be plugged. Since the Z8603 has pin arrangements identical to those of the Z8601 it can be plugged into a socket in the final system to test the rest of the hardware and the program. It is also a convenient way to build low-volume systems since there is no need for the delays inherent in mask design and programming; the user needs only a facility for programming the widely used 2716 EPROM.

Although add-with-carry and subtract-with-carry instructions are provided to enable multiple length arithmetic to be performed, there are no general 16-bit registers provided, and only the jump and call (subroutine) instructions provide for 16-bit operands or addresses. The only 16-bit register included is the program counter. The instruction set thus differs from that of the Z80, being more suitable for control applications than complex calculations.

For applications requiring more program space, variants of the Z8601, Z8602 and Z8603 are available. These provide 4K bytes of ROM, but are otherwise similar and are designated Z8611, Z8612 and Z8613.

5.5   The Motorola MC6801

The 8048 family and the Z8601 are both provided with reduced instruction sets and different architecture compared with earlier 8-bit microprocessors produced by the same manufacturers (the 8080 and the Z80).

An alternative strategy was used by Motorola, who decided that program compatibility was a useful feature. In consequence their single-chip microprocessor uses the full M6800 instruction set with a number of enhancements. In a 40-pin package it includes an M6800 processor, 2K bytes of mask ROM, 128 bytes of RAM, a 16-bit timer, a serial communications interface and 31 parallel I/O lines, together with $\overline{IRQ}$ and $\overline{NMI}$ interrupt lines. As with other single-chip microprocessors the clock circuits are included, and only a crystal is needed external to the chip.

In addition to the single-chip mode, the MC6801 can be used with expanded I/O when port 3 provides 8 data lines and port 4 provides 8 address lines. Where more address space is needed, multiplexed operation can be used. For this the lower address lines A0−A7 are multiplexed with the data at port 3 and port 4 supplies the high address lines A8−A15. The control line SC1 then acts as an address strobe in the same way as the ALE signal on Intel 8085 and 8048 processors. The choice of operating mode is decided by the logic levels wired to pins 8, 9 and 10. These are read into the processor via port 2 during the $\overline{RESET}$ period and if external I/O is used on port 2 it must be isolated during the $\overline{RESET}$ pulse. The levels on pins 8, 9 and 10 allow either internal or external ROM or RAM to be selected, and also provide test facilities to enable the contents of ROM and RAM to be transferred to port 3.

Because the four I/O ports are fabricated on the chip, their addresses are fixed according to the following table

Port no.	Data address	Data direction register address
1	0002	0000
2	0003	0001
3	0006	0004
4	0007	0005

These addresses respond in exactly the same way as the 6820 PIA registers, but they are all directly accessible since they have separate addresses rather than sharing one address as in the 6820.

The only port which has a control register is port 3. This controls the input strobe SC1, the output strobe SC2, and also the ability of SC1 to interrupt the processor. The MS bit acts as an interrupt flag bit.

The processor hardware is expanded from that of the M6800 by the inclusion of a few extra instructions to perform 16-bit arithmetic on a notional 16-bit accumulator D formed by concatenating the A and B accumulators. The only 16-bit operations are ADD (from two successive store locations), LOAD, SHIFT, STORE and SUBTRACT. There is also a hardware multiply feature which multiplies the two 8-bit numbers held in accumulators A and B, and deposits the 16-bit product in accumulator D.

These enhancements will considerably increase the processing speed for any arithmetic operations where 8-bit numbers alone do not provide sufficient accuracy.

For program and hardware development the manufacturers provide the MC68701 and the MC6801P1. The MC68701 is identical to the MC6801 but has an EPROM in place of ROM for program storage. It is thus also convenient for low-volume applications. The MC6801P1 is compatible with the MC6801 as regards processor, I/O ports and instruction set, but its internal 2K ROM contains a debug monitor program which enables a program to be loaded via the serial cassette tape interface into external RAM, and the user can then insert breakpoints, examine instructions and register contents, or single step the program. When debugged and verified the program can be dumped on to tape.

This chip is used in the complete MC6801 Microcomputer Evaluation Module which allows systems to be assembled, then programmed and tested via a computer terminal.

A variant of the MC6801 is the MC6803, which has the same enhanced instruction set, a UART for serial I/O, a timer, port A (8 bits) and port B (5 bits). The remaining I/O lines are arranged as 8 multiplexed data (D0–D7) and address (A0–A7) lines, 8 high-order address lines (A8–A15) and an address strobe. The latter line acts like the ALE signal of an 8085 to latch the low-order address lines.

The MC6803 is intended for systems which need more than 2K bytes of programs, and can be expanded to handle 64K program bytes. Like earlier processors it has 128 bytes of RAM and clock circuits on the chip.

There are many other single-chip microprocessors on the market, but only a short account of the most widely used devices will be given.

6 Practical Problems and Applications

6.1 Sensing Data from Mechanical Switches

Many of the input signals needed by microprocessor systems are derived from mechanical switches or contacts. At first sight there appears to be no difficulty in connecting these devices to a PIA port; for example all port inputs can be connected via pull-up resistors to the +5 V supply, and the switch can be connected between a data line and earth. The normal condition is then that all inputs are high, and when one or more goes low, a switch has been operated. If processor action is required, all inputs could be connected to an AND gate as shown in figure 6.1, and the output used either to set a flag or create an interrupt. A service routine could then read the port, determine which line was earthed, store this fact and return from the service routine. One possible action would be to increment a counter keeping a running total of the number of operations of a set of contacts.

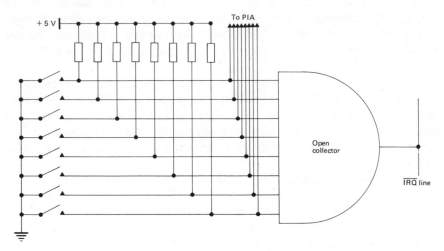

Figure 6.1 Creating an interrupt from switch operation

Unfortunately, such a simple arrangement would almost invariably result in serious errors, each switch action producing several interrupts. In order to discover the reason for this, the electrical output of the switch must be examined in fine detail. Nearly all switches and relays suffer from 'contact bounce', that is, the contacts bounce against one another several times before establishing permanent contact. This is of little consequence when they are used to control lamps, motors, relays, etc., because these devices have comparatively long time constants. However, a simple interrupt service routine may last no longer than 100 μs, whereas switch or relay contacts may continue bouncing for several milliseconds. Thus each momentary contact may be treated by the processor as a separate switch operation, so producing errors.

Several methods of overcoming this problem can be used, depending upon circumstances. Probably the cheapest is a software solution; in this the program senses the first momentary contact in the normal way and then enters a short delay loop. The delay is usually 4–7 ms, somewhat longer than the time during which the contacts may be bouncing. The state of the contacts is sensed again, and if they are still closed this is taken to be a genuine switch operation which is acted upon. The switch subsequently must remain open for the same period before this information is accepted. Thus no further switch closure will be taken as valid until the contacts have remained closed for, say 5 ms and subsequently remained open for a further 5 ms.

Some similar action is needed even if the switch signal sets a flag in a control register, for example, by operating on one of the control lines of an M6820 PIA. Although repeated transitions cannot affect the flag once it has been set, if the service routine is entered quickly it may sense the flag state, act upon it, clear the flag ready for the next transition and end the service routine in 100 μs or so, before the contacts have finished bouncing. Here again a delay can be interposed between sensing the flag state and clearing it ready to sense the next transition.

A mechanical method of avoiding contact bounce can be applied to relays by using mercury-wetted contacts, but this is a very expensive solution and one that cannot be applied if the switches are already installed and the microprocessor is required to use their output as best it can.

A hardware solution can be used in which each switch is followed by a bistable, as shown in figure 6.2. This however needs a changeover switch which may not always be available. Where only a make or a break contact is provided, its output can be used to trigger a monostable. If this is set for a pulse length of 5 ms, no further switch signals will be recognised until after this delay time and a further recovery period have elapsed.

The cheapest hardware solution is to put a C–R circuit having a time constant of, say 50 ms in series with the switch signal. This will ensure that the signal fed to the microprocessor cannot reach the logic threshold (typically 2.5 V) until well after the contacts have stopped bouncing. Thus the input signal will be monotonic near the logic threshold and there will be no possibility of multiple operations being caused by a single switch action. The main disadvantage of this scheme is that it causes a longer delay in signal recognition than any other method.

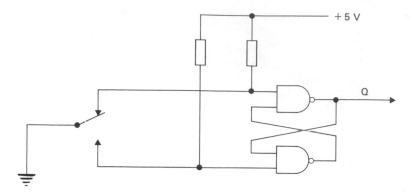

Figure 6.2 Using a bistable to remove switch transients

6.2 Manual Input Devices

Many microprocessor systems are required to accept manual inputs of a few quantities which can in most cases be entered in a digital form. Where the information is not expected to change very often, a rotary or thumbwheel switch is convenient, since its position stores the data, and it can be interrogated by the microprocessor at any time. Where more information is required, or is changed at more frequent intervals, a keyboard is often preferred. The input rate is higher, but as each key is pressed only momentarily the data must be captured immediately and stored within the microprocessor system.

We first examine the input of data from thumbwheel switches. These are generally fitted with printed circuit switch wafers which are coded in BCD format to output either direct or negated signals.

Where the peripheral package has internal pull-up resistors, no further components need be used if the moving contacts are earthed and the other four contacts are taken to four input lines. The A port of the 6821 PIA has this feature, but most other packages need external resistors.

Where manual input is used, numerical data will almost invariably be in decimal notation, and the first task of any input program is usually to convert the data to binary notation so that the normal arithmetic instructions can be used.

Program 6.1 is not a completely general one in that it concerns only positive values; it reads three BCD thumbswitches and converts the number encoded into an 8-bit binary value. The maximum input number which can be handled correctly is 255, more than adequate for the particular application, but if all values up to 999 are valid, double length working will be required.

The three switches are connected to a 6821 PIA in a M6800 microprocessor system and occupy 12 bits, in this case all of port A and half (bits 0–3) of

Program 6.1 To Read BCD Switches and Convert Data to Binary Code

Location	Instruction		Code	Comment
				Conversion subroutine. X and Y in the 4 LS bits of ACC A and ACC B, remaining 4 bits are zero.
0010	CONV:	ASLA	48	Generates 2X
11		PSH A	36	Push 2X on to stack
12		ASLA	48	4X
13		ASLA	48	8X
14		ABA	1B	8X + Y
15		PULB	33	Fetch 2X
16		ABA	1B	10X + Y now in ACC A
17		RTS	39	Return to main program
0020	SETUP:	LDA A # 04	86	Set up PIAs for data
21			04	Loads bit pattern in ACC A
22		STA A CRA	B7	Load CRA
23			40	
24			01	
25		STA A CRB	B7	and CRB
26			40	
27			03	
28	START:	LDA A PA	B6	Read input switches
29			40	ACC A
2A			00	T | U
2B		PSH A	26	Copy on to stack
2C		PSH A	36	Copy on to stack
2D		LDA A PB	B6	Fetch hundreds digit
2E			40	into ACC A
2F			02	
0030		AND A # 0F	84	Mask off 4 MS bits
31			0F	
32		PUL B	33	Fetch tens and units digits
33		LSR B	54	Shift tens digit down
34		LSR B	54	to 4 LS bits
35		LSR B	54	ready for
36		LSR B	54	conversion
37		JSR CONV	BD	Jump to CONV
38			00	Subroutine giving
39			10	10H + T in ACC A
3A		PUL B	33	Fetch tens and units digits
3B		AND B # 0F	C4	Mask off units digit
3C			0F	in 4 LS bits
3D		JSR CONV	BD	Jump to CONV
3E			00	Subroutine, leaving
3F			10	100H + 10T + U in ACC A
0040		STA A 00	97	Store result in
41			00	loc. 0000
42		HALT	3F	Halt

port B. This means that only the 4 bits on port B (the hundreds digit) will require external pull-up resistors. The bit allocation is as follows

		PB					PA		
7 6 5 4	3 2 1 0	7 6 5 4	3 2 1 0
	Hundreds	Tens	Units

The technique adopted is to use nested multiplication, that is to evaluate

$$BIN = 100\,(H) + 10\,(T) + U$$

where H, T and U are the hundreds, tens and units digits; we write it in the form

$$BIN = 10\,(10H + T) + U$$

Thus if we write a subroutine to generate from two numbers X and Y the expression $10X + Y$, we can invoke it twice. The first time we insert for X and Y the numbers H and T, and the second time the result of the first calculation and U. It is convenient to start with X in ACC A and Y in ACC B. The subroutine starting in location 10 uses an arithmetic shift left of ACC A to generate 2X. This is stored on the stack and shifted two further places left to generate 8X. Adding ACC B generates $8X + Y$, and as we no longer need the contents of ACC B we can pull 2X from the stack into it. A final addition of ACC B to ACC A leaves the value $10X + Y$ in ACC A.

The main program then consists of a set-up segment which initialises the PIA registers, and a main segment which reads the data from each port in turn, masks unwanted bits out and moves the digit information into the accumulators. The subroutine is invoked twice, leaving the result in ACC A, and a copy in location 0000.

In order to isolate each digit, a masking operation is performed which clears the four MS bits and leaves the required digit in the four LS bits. The logical AND instruction with an immediate operand 0F (0000 1111) performs this task in locations 0030 and 003B.

The program is written to follow a power-on reset, so that the control registers and data direction registers of the PIA are all cleared. Both ports A and B are then programmed as inputs. The control word entered into CRA and CRB serves only to permit access to the data ports PA and PB, and allows no interrupts.

The program is initially entered at location 0020, to set up the PIA registers; thereafter it is entered at location 0028 to read the data and convert it to binary form. Most of the main program starting at 0028 is concerned with moving the data and masking them, locating them in accumulators A and B prior to calling the CONV subroutine.

Since the stack is used for temporary storage the initialising segment of the processor program must load the stack pointer with a suitable address within the RAM address space.

The addresses used in the program for the PIA registers are

4000	PA/DDRA
4001	CRA
4002	PB/DDRB
4003	CRB

6.3   Input from Keyboards

Keyboards are operated only momentarily and so data must be captured as soon as they appear on the keyboard. The input arrangements are thus much different from those suitable for switches which can be read at any convenient time.

One possible technique would be to connect one pole of each switch of the keyboard to, say +5 V. The other pole could be connected to an input line, and any closed switch would generate a 1 in the input data. While this gives a simple method of deducing which key has been pressed it is extravagant in the use of peripheral packages. An 8-way keyboard needs only one port, but a full type-writer keyboard having around 50 keys would need three or more packages. In order to reduce the number of I/O lines, and so the interfacing cost, most keyboards are connected in matrix form. In this a set of wires is connected to the I/O pins and located in two groups of column and row lines which are mutually at right angles. Each switch is then wired between a column and a row line, one at each intersection. The arrangement is shown in figure 6.3.

In this method only $(m + n)$ lines to the I/O ports are needed for scanning $m \times n$ keys, for example 12 lines for 32 keys, or 14 lines for 48 keys. By using decoders some further reduction in the number of I/O lines can be made.

As an example figure 6.3 shows a 4×8 matrix keyboard. In order to determine which key has been operated the following bit patterns are sent to the four output lines

0	1	1	1
1	0	1	1
1	1	0	1
1	1	1	0

After each output, the input port is read, and the resulting byte is transferred to an accumulator. If it contains a zero, this will indicate the column in which the selected key is located, if not the next output is generated. If the zero is found after outputting the first pattern, with zero in the lefthand bit, the selected key lies in the first row; if after outputting the second pattern 1011, it lies in the second row, and so on.

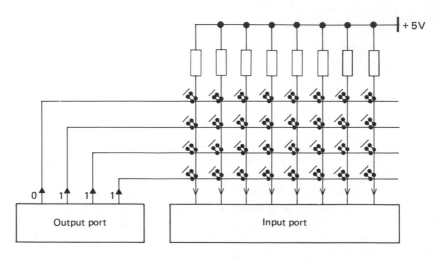

Figure 6.3 Keyboard scanning circuit

The column can easily be found by rotating the byte through the carry bit and counting how many operations are needed to reach the zero.

The existence of a zero can be determined by complementing the byte and using the BEQ or JRZ (branch if equal to zero, or jump relative if zero) instruction to advance to the next bit pattern if all bits are zero. As soon as this test fails, a 1 has been found in the byte corresponding to the column signals, resulting from a zero in the original byte before complementing.

For completeness the byte should be rotated eight times and, if more than one 1 is found, the program can branch to an error routine since two keys have been pressed simultaneously.

In the same way all four bit patterns must be output to ensure that only one key is pressed. If two different output patterns both produce a 0 in the byte read from the columns, two keys are being pressed.

A simple procedure for dealing with the error is to return to the start of the scanning operation and continue scanning until only one key is pressed. This process is more effective if the correct detection of a key depression is followed by an audible signal to indicate to the operator that the next character can be sent.

6.4   Reverse Scanning

A simple procedure which needs only two I/O operations can be used if the groups of lines connected to the rows and columns can easily be switched from sending to receiving. The method is shown in figure 6.4 applied to a 16-way keyboard, using a single port, in this case port PA of a 6821 PIA attached to a M6800 microprocessor. Both row and column lines need pull-up resistors, since they are used in turn as inputs. If connected to port A, internal pull-up resistors are provided, but external resistors are shown in figure 6.4 as they are required if port B, or a different type of peripheral package, is used.

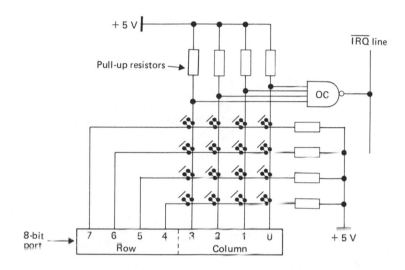

Figure 6.4 Reverse keyboard scanning

The procedure adopted is to identify the column connected to the selected key, and then energise this column only. The row can then be determined, so identifying the particular key pressed. Program 6.2 handles the commands to the PIA and the detection of the key which has been pressed. The program is written so that it can be used either as a subroutine, or part of an interrupt service routine.

The first action required is to clear the control register, so giving access to the data direction register which shares address 4000 with the data port PA. The control register address is 4001. The DDR is loaded via accumulator A with the bit pattern 1111 0000 (F0 in hexadecimal), so programming bits PA0–3 as inputs and PA4–7 as outputs. The control register is then loaded with 04, so switching access to the data port.

Program 6.2 To Handle Commands to PIA and Detect Key Pressed

Location	Instruction	Code	Comment
0010	START: CLR CRA	7F	Clear CRA for access
11		40	to DDRA
12		01	
13	LDA A # F0	86	Load bit pattern
14		F0	for DDRA
15	STA A DDRA	B7	Set PA0–3 as input
16		40	PA4–7 as output
17		00	
18	LDA A # 04	86	Load bit pattern for access
19		04	to PA
1A	STA A CRA	B7	Output to CRA
1B		40	
1C		01	
1D	LDA A # 0F	86	Clear 4 MS bits
1E		0F	
1F	STA A PA	B7	Output to PA
0020		40	drives row line low
21		00	
22	LDA A PA	B6	Read resulting data
23		40	giving selected column
24		00	
25	CLR CRA	7F	Set switch for
26		40	access to DDRA
27		01	
28	COM DDRA	73	Exchange inputs
29		40	and outputs
2A		00	
2B	LDA B # 04	C6	Load bit pattern
2C		04	for access to PA
2D	STA B CRA	F7	Output to CRA
2E		40	
2F		01	
0030	STA A PA	B7	Output 0 on selected
31		40	column
32		00	
33	LDA A PA	B6	Read back final
34		40	data, giving row selected
35		00	
36	CLR B	5F	Clear ACC B for key counter
37	LDX # TABLE	CE	Load starting address
38		00	of table into
39		50	index register
3A	SERCH: CMPA X, 0	A1	Compare final data
3B		00	with entry in table
3C	BEQ LOAD	27	Branch to LOAD if
3D		09	match found

3E		INC B	5C	Increment key counter
3F		INX	08	Increment address
0040		CPX #TABEND	8C	Compare address with
41			00	TABEND (0060)
42			60	
43		BEQ START	27	If table searched
44			CB	start again
45		BRA SERCH	20	If more bytes to compare
46			F3	continue searching
47	LOAD:	STA B 00	D7	Store key number
48			00	in location 00
49		HLT	3F	Halt
4A				
4B				

Data table

0050	TABLE: —	77	Key	0
51		7B		1
52		7D		2
53		7E		3
54		B7		4
55		BB		5
56		BD		6
57		BE		7
58		D7		8
59		DB		9
5A		DD		A
5B		DE		B
5C		E7		C
5D		ED		D
5E		ED		E
5F		EE		F

0060	TABEND:

Four zeros are then sent to PA4–7, and four ones to PA0–3 by loading accumulator A with 0F and sending this to PA. This outputs earth potential to the four row lines. If any key is depressed the corresponding column line will now be pulled down to earth. Consequently, the four bits PA0–3 will be forced to one of the following bit patterns

Pattern	Column earthed
0111	3
1011	2
1101	1
1110	0

The column has now been identified, and the inputs and outputs can now be reversed, storing the column information in accumulator A meanwhile. The control register is again cleared, to permit access to the DDR, which is complemented. This now sets PA0–3 as outputs and PA4–7 as inputs. The immediate operand 04 is now loaded into accumulator B and output to the control register, so switching access back to PA. A bit pattern containing the column information in bits PA0–3 and four ones in PA4–7 is next sent from accumulator A to port PA, so earthing the selected column. The port is now read back into accumulator A, and it will contain information giving both the row and column number of the key pressed, according to the following table

Row no.	*Column no.*	*Bit pattern* PA7–4 (row); PA3–0 (column)
3	7	0 1 1 1
2	6	1 0 1 1
1	5	1 1 0 1
0	4	1 1 1 0

The decoding process to find which key was pressed is now started. This involves holding a set of all 16 possible patterns in the store, and comparing the pattern held in accumulator A with each in turn. Accumulator B is first cleared to act as a counter, and is incremented after each comparison. The index register is loaded with the starting address of the table and, after each comparison, it is incremented and compared with the address immediately following the table. If no comparison has been successful the conclusion is that two keys are pressed, and scanning continues until only one is held down. When this happens a match will be found and the key number is loaded into location 00 and the program ends.

If a message is being input, the program may return to the beginning of the segment given and continue searching for additional characters until either a fixed number have been accepted, or until a particular character signifying the end of data has been accepted, for example, a letter if only decimal data are valid.

An alternative would be to use interrupts. This involves executing only the seven instructions down to the first STA A PA operation. This puts a low logic level on all four row lines PA4–7. The program can then proceed to other tasks until a key is pressed. When this occurs one of the four column lines will be pulled down to earth, so giving a logic 0 output from the NAND gate and creating an interrupt.

The bit pattern sent to the control register will need changing to allow an interrupt. If CA1 is used, it must set the control flag on the rising edge of the waveform, so that the control word sent to CRA in location 4001 must be 0000 0111 or 07 (hexadecimal).

Both this method and the previous one take no account of the possibility of contact bounce. In order to avoid trouble from this both of the programs should start with a delay of 4–7 ms before any scanning action begins. This ensures that all bouncing is finished before any switch state is tested.

6.5 Driving Digital Displays

Microprocessors are frequently required to produce output in a form which the user can read easily. Where this is in numerical form an illuminated display is particularly convenient as it can be read at a distance despite considerable variations in ambient lighting. Light-emitting diodes are widely used for this purpose on account of their long life, robustness and low driving voltage, and in particular the 7-segment version which can display all of the figures and a number of letters including those used in hexadecimal notation.

The segments are positioned as shown in figure 6.5, and labelled a–g when viewed from the front. Each segment requires a current of 10–20 mA, depending on size, at a potential of 1.3–1.7 V. The current cannot be supplied by a standard parallel I/O package, and a transistor driver per segment is needed. Displays can be obtained with either a common anode or a common cathode, but in either case a total current of 70 mA or more will flow when all segments are illuminated.

Where only one or two digits are to be displayed, each segment can be connected via a driver transistor to one line of an output port. However, if six digits are to be displayed, for example, this arrangement needs three parallel I/O packages together with 42 transistors and is thus expensive.

The number of I/O lines can be greatly reduced by multiplexing the displays. This involves energising only one display at a time, and so the same set of 7-segment lines can be used for all displays. If we assume that common cathode displays are used, the display to be illuminated is selected by switching its cathode to earth potential, while maintaining all other cathodes at +5 V. The segments to be illuminated are connected via a current-limiting resistor and a driver transistor (turned fully on) to the +5 V supply.

With this arrangement we need only 7 lines for segment drive and 1 per display, that is 15 for an 8-digit display compared with 56 lines if multiplexing is not used. Since only one display is turned on at a time, a 3-to-8 wire decoder could be used to select the display energised, so needing only 3 wires for digit selection, or 10 wires in all.

A typical arrangement is shown in figure 6.5. Note that for a mean current per segment of say 7 mA, since each digit is turned on for about a quarter of the time, the current during conduction must be in the region of 30 mA.

The value of the limiting resistor connected between the segment line and the driver transistor must be chosen accordingly.

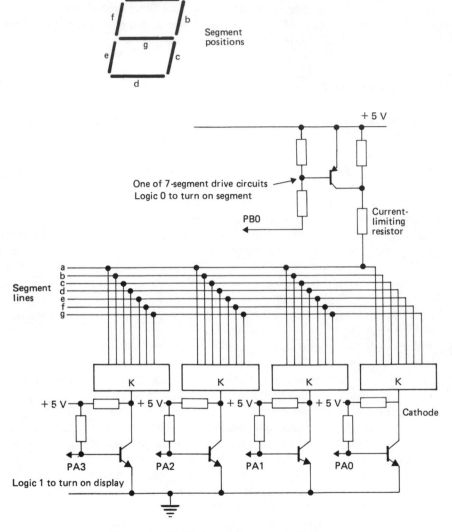

Figure 6.5 Multiplexed 7-segment display

In order to illustrate the way in which multiplexed displays can be controlled we take as an example a four-digit display in which segments a–g are connected via p–n–p driver transistors to lines PB0–PB6 of a parallel I/O package attached to a M6800 microcomputer. A 0 level on one of these lines will turn on the corresponding segment. The individual cathodes are taken via n–p–n driver transistors to lines PA0–3 to select one display at a time. The lines PA4–7 are not used and in this program are loaded with 0; PA0–3 are initially loaded with 1000 to select the lefthand display. A logical shift right will change this to 0100 so selecting the next display. The order of actions is as follows

> Turn off all segments
> Select next display
> Select next digit pattern
> Output to segment drives
> Enter short delay loop
> Repeat if more digits to display

It is important to turn off all segments before selecting the next display, otherwise some unwanted segments will be illuminated momentarily. This gives a faint 'ghosting' effect and reduces the contrast of the displays.

The segment connections are as follows

Segment	a	b	c	d	e	f	g
PB line	0	1	2	3	4	5	6

Thus to display 1, segments b and c must be illuminated, so requiring a bit pattern with 0 for bits 1 and 2 and 1 elsewhere. PB7 is not used and is programmed as a zero. The bit pattern is then 0111 1001 or 79 (hexadecimal). Similarly, for 0, segments a, b, c, d, e and f must be illuminated. This requires a bit pattern 0100 0000 or 40. The remaining digits require the following bit patterns

Digit	Bit patterns (hexadecimal)
2	24
3	30
4	19
5	12
6	02
7	78
8	00
9	10
A	08
B	03
C	46
D	21
E	06
F	0E
Blank	7F

Program 6.3 handles only the display action, and consists of a data area

Program 6.3 To Display 4 Characters with Multiplexed Display

Location	Instruction	Code	Comment
0000		79	Bit pattern for 1
01		24	Bit pattern for 2
02		30	Bit pattern for 3
03		19	Bit pattern for 4
04	DELAY: LDA A #65	86	Delay subroutine − load
05		65	constant for 1 ms delay
06	LP: DEC A	4A	Decrement ACC A
07	BNE LP	26	Repeat if not zero
08		FD	
09	RTS	39	Return to main program
0A			
0010	COM DDRA	73	Complement DDRA
11		40	to switch PA for output
12		00	
13	COM DDRB	73	Complement DDRB
14		40	to switch PD for output
15		02	
16	LDA A #04	86	Load bit pattern for access
17		04	to PA into ACC A
18	STA A CRA	B7	Transfer to CRA
19		40	
1A		01	
1B	STA A CRB	B7	Transfer to CRB
1C		40	
1D		03	This ends set up
1E	START: LDA B #08	C6	Load bit pattern to
1F		08	select LH digit
0020	LDX #0000	CE	Load address of first
21		00	character into index
22		00	register
23	LOOP: CLR PB	7F	Turn off all segments
24		40	
25		02	
26	LDA A X, 0	A6	Fetch next character
27		00	
28	INX	08	
29	STA B PA	F7	Select display
2A		40	to be energised
2B		00	
2C	LSR B	54	Shift pattern for next digit
2D	STA A PB	B7	Output data to segment
2E		40	lines to display digit
2F		02	
0030	JSR DELAY	BD	Jump to delay subroutine
31	TST B	5D	Have four digits been displayed?
32	BNE LOOP	26	No, get next
33		EF	digit
34	BRA START	20	Yes, go back to repeat
35		E8	the display

00—03 in which the patterns for the four digits to be displayed are held, the delay subroutine in locations 04—09, the PIA initialising routine in 10—1D and the main program in 1E—35. For a continuous display the section 1E—35 must be repeated as shown in this program, but any additional action lasting no more than a few milliseconds could be added to the loop. The program is for running after a power-on reset in which all PIA registers have been cleared.

In order to avoid confusion between figures and letters the figure 6 has a horizontal top, using segment a, and letters B and D are displayed in lower case. Some care is needed when reading the display to distinguish between 6 and b, but this occurs only with hexadecimal notation, during program development and testing. The displays are normally restricted to decimal numbers only for the end user, and confusion is avoided.

The program must continually refresh the display, but there is also time to scan a keyboard, and count incoming pulses or some similar task involving say a few milliseconds of processor action every 20 or so milliseconds.

The initialising needs to be performed once only; the rest of the program is here shown as an infinite loop, but there would usually be an extra section inserted for scanning a keyboard; or examining some input channel. Exit from the loop is usually caused by pressing a particular key or set of keys, or by an external interrupt.

The 1 ms delay routine is written for the D2 development system which has a 614 kHz clock signal. Thus the routine must occupy 614 clock cycles in all. Since a development system was used, the entire program is held in RAM, but in the final version all of the program apart from the four characters to be displayed would be in some form of ROM and located nearer the top of the address space.

In many situations the input to the program might be the numerical values of the digits, in which case a table look-up process is needed. This can be performed by including a table of the bit pattern for each digit, and setting the index register to the address of the first entry. An accumulator is cleared for use as a counter, and its contents compared with the digit. If there is no match, the counter and the index register are incremented and a further match is tried. This is repeated until a match is found, when the index register will contain the address of the bit pattern needed to display the digit concerned. This procedure could precede the display of each digit, but some time can be saved at the cost of a little more program if the table look-up is performed once only, and the resulting bit patterns are then used to load locations 00—03 of program 6.3.

6.6 Waveform Generation

A requirement which often arises in microprocessor-controlled test equipment and some other applications is the generation of a particular waveform of voltage as a function of time. Usually the method adopted is to connect a D/A converter to output port or ports and send a sequence of digital values. These may be computed or stored internally. Unless the waveform is a relatively slow one, there is no time for complex calculations and the values are best read from the store. The following example, program 6.4, runs on a Z80 micro-processor with an 8-bit D/A converter attached to port 05.

The waveform is that of a biased sinewave represented by

$$v = V_0 k(1 + \sin \theta)$$

since the DAC can supply only a positive output signal. The scale factor V_0 is 10 mV/bit so that k has a value of 128 and the output changes from 0 to 2.55 V. For a sinusoidal waveform, since the output is symmetrical, the DAC output can be taken through a capacitor to eliminate the d.c. component and provide only the sinusoidal component.

The frequency can be altered by putting a variable delay after each sample has been sent to the DAC.

The program starts with sending the control byte 0F to port 07, which is the control register for the data port 05. This programs port 05 for byte output. The HL register is then loaded with the starting address of the data, and register B with the number of data samples, in this case 32_{10} or 20 (hexadecimal). The main loop then fetches a byte of data into the accumulator, outputs it to

Program 6.4 For Waveform Generation

Location	Instruction	Code	Comment
CE0	LDA # 0F	3E	Fetch bit pattern to set
1		0F	port A for output
2	OUT CRA	D3	Output to control register
3		07	
4	START: LD HL # 0D00	21	Load HL with starting
5		00	address of data block
6		0D	
7	LD B # 20	06	Load B with number of
8		20	bytes of data
9	LOOP: LDA, (HL)	7E	Fetch next data byte
A	OUT 05	D3	Output to DAC
B		05	
C	INC HL	23	Increment address pointer
D	DEC B	05	Decrement byte count
E	JRNZ LOOP	28	Repeat if not finished
F		F9	
CF0	JR START	18	If end of cycle return
1		F2	to START

Data for Generating $y = 128(1 + \sin \theta)$

Location	Instruction	Code	Comment
0D00		80	$\theta = 0°$
1		99	$\theta = 11\frac{1}{4}°$
2		B1	$\theta = 22\frac{1}{2}°$
3		C7	
4		DA	
5		EA	
6		F6	
7		FE	
8		FF	$\theta = 90°$
9		FE	
A		F6	
B		EA	
C		DA	
D		C7	
E		B1	
F		99	
0D10		80	$\theta = 180°$
1		67	
2		4F	
3		39	
4		26	
5		16	
6		A	
7		2	
8		1	$\theta = 270°$
9		2	
A		A	
B		16	
C		26	
D		39	
E		4F	
F		67	
0D20			
1			
2			

the DAC via port 05, increments HL, decrements B and repeats the process until B is reduced to zero. A complete cycle of data has then been transmitted and the program returns to the beginning to repeat the process. The program stores the function $y = 128 (1 + \sin \theta)$ for a complete cycle, with $11\frac{1}{2}°$ increments of θ, except that the peak of the waveform is reduced to 255 (= FF) since this is the largest unsigned number that can be held in an 8-bit register. For symmetry the minimum value is coded as 1 instead of 0. The resulting waveform has a total of 32 steps in a complete cycle and a lowpass filter will remove much of the energy introduced by the step changes of level. The result is an approximation to a sinewave which is acceptable for many purposes.

If storage space is restricted only a quarter of the data points need to be stored and the remainder can be deduced from them. However, this is possible only for a waveform with the degree of symmetry which the sinewave possesses; other waveforms generally need the storage of a complete cycle of data.

7   Microcomputer Buses

7.1   The Development of Standard Buses

When microprocessors first appeared there was no general agreement among manufacturers about power supplies, logic levels, or the number and functions of the control signals. Later, with the adoption of n-channel devices it became possible to use the same +5 V power supply as had been standardised for TTL packages. The industry-wide standards for TTL and CMOS logic were extended to peripheral computer packages such as RAM, ROM and EPROM devices, but not to the central microprocessor package itself.

As microprocessors became more widely used there arose a need for simple methods of system expansion by adding more data and program storage and additional peripheral devices such as teleprinters, A/D and D/A converters, CRT displays, keyboards, etc. The cost of these, if a separate design were required for every microprocessor type, was prohibitive, and the market did not expand rapidly until one manufacturer proposed a specification and pin layout for a bus system which could be used with a wide range of microprocessors. This was the S–100 bus which became an industry standard. Subsequently other manufacturers produced different designs of bus which were adopted as national and in some cases international standards. The following sections give a short account of the more important of these.

7.2   The S–100 Bus

This bus was introduced by MITS Inc. in the USA as a feature of their Altair 8800 kit. This used an 8080 processor, so that the bus signals largely follow the arrangements for data, address and control signals of the 8080. The 100 ways on the bus connector mate with a double-sided printed circuit plug which has a contact spacing of 0.125 inch.

The original specification was inadequate in some respects in that no specific uses were prescribed for 19 of the lines, and the timing of the various waveforms could vary considerably. The consequence was that one could not guarantee that any S–100 board would work satisfactorily with any other S–100 board. The resulting dissatisfaction led the IEEE in the USA to propose a tighter specification which would ensure compatibility between all S–100 boards. Although other microprocessor bus standards have been proposed, the S–100 is at present the one most widely used with many hundreds of different types of board being available from over a hundred manufacturers. Although originally intended to work with an 8080 microprocessor, it has a number of lines which do not connect directly to the processor chip. One feature which differs from many other bus arrangements is the power supply provision. Only unregulated d.c. supplies are provided, +8 V and ±16 V, and each board needs a local regulator to provide fully stabilised supplies. This limits the damage to a single board if a regulator fails, and avoids allocating 4—6 pins or more to power lines to minimise voltage drop if a central regulator is used. Unfortunately earth, +8 V and −16 V are allocated to three adjacent pins. This can very easily cause damage to integrated circuits and power supplies if a board is removed or inserted with power on. Also the clock signals are placed next to slower signal lines and can easily induce noise into them. One manufacturer interposes an earth line between each two adjacent signal lines on the back plane board to reduce cross-talk. This is standard practice in many minicomputer bus cables.

Since all current microprocessors are designed for bidirectional data lines, the use of two separate 8-bit data buses, one for input and the other for output, is an unexpected feature of the S—100 bus. The two buses are connected in parallel to the microprocessor, but are otherwise separated. There is no need for separate buses, but the arrangement simplifies the use of buffers in the bus lines. This odd feature however was turned to good use with the advent of 16-bit microprocessors, since the 16 data lines could then be operated as a bidirectional 16-bit bus. Two handshaking lines are allocated for this action, $\overline{\text{SXTRQ}}$ a 16-bit request issued by the bus master, and $\overline{\text{SXTN}}$ generated by 16-bit slaves in reply. When the reply has been received, the master is enabled to send a 16-bit data word, the DO (data out) lines carrying the low byte and the DI (data in) lines the high byte.

The terminology resembles that of the PDP—11 Unibus designed by Digital Equipment Corporation, in that transactions occur between the bus master (usually the microprocessor) and a slave. Four DMA (direct memory access) lines with priority adjudication are provided. Using these a peripheral device can assume bus mastership for communicating directly with the store or with another peripheral. Three lines are not defined and can be used for any purpose the manufacturer requires, and four are reserved for future use (RFU) and must not be allocated by a manufacturer. Most 16-bit microprocessors can handle more address space than the 64K bytes accessible from a 16-bit address bus; consequently the S—100 bus now provides eight more extended address lines A16—A23 to give a total of 24 address lines.

The bus is arranged to handle an 8-input interrupt controller which has inputs on the VI0 to VI7 lines. The controller determines which interrupt request has highest priority, and puts its vector address on the data bus when the processor asserts s INTA.

Table 7.1 gives a list of the line allocations in the revised S—100 bus (IEEE). The lines are shown as direct (1 = high potential) or negated, for example,

Table 7.1 S–100 Bus Signals

Pin no.	Signal	Description
1	+8 V	Unregulated supply for +5 V regulators
2	+16 V	Unregulated supply
3	$\overline{\text{XRDY}}$ (S)	Allows slaves to hold up processor until they are ready
4	$\overline{\text{VI0}}$ (S)	
5	$\overline{\text{VI1}}$ (S)	8 vector interrupt lines. $\overline{\text{VI0}}$ has
6	$\overline{\text{VI2}}$ (S)	highest priority. Should be open
7	$\overline{\text{VI3}}$ (S)	collector drivers
8	$\overline{\text{VI4}}$ (S)	$\overline{\text{VI7}}$ has lowest priority
9	$\overline{\text{VI5}}$ (S)	
10	$\overline{\text{VI6}}$ (S)	
11	$\overline{\text{VI7}}$ (S)	
12	$\overline{\text{NMI}}$ (S)	Non-maskable interrupt. Open collector
13	$\overline{\text{PWRFAIL}}$	Pulled low when loss of power is sensed. Must be asserted at least 50 ms before the local regulators lose control. Used for automatic saving of register contents
14	$\overline{\text{DMA3}}$	Highest priority DMA request line. Open collector
15	A18 (M)	Extended address line 18
16	A16 (M)	Extended address line 16
17	A17 (M)	Extended address line 17
18	$\overline{\text{SDSB}}$ (M)	Status disable. Puts the 8 status lines into a high impedance state. Open collector
19	$\overline{\text{CDSB}}$ (M)	Command disable. Puts the 6 command/control lines into a high impedance state. Open collector
20	EARTH	
21	NDEF	Not defined in standard
22	$\overline{\text{ADSB}}$ (M)	Address disable. Puts the 24 address lines into a high impedance state. Open collector
23	$\overline{\text{DODSB}}$ (M)	Data out disable. Puts 8 data out lines into a high impedance state
24	Ø	Master timing for the bus, generally the microprocessor clock signal
25	p $\overline{\text{STVAL}}$ (M)	Status valid strobe. Indicates that status information may be sampled
26	p HLDA (M)	Hold acknowledge. Signals to the highest priority device seeking bus control that the permanent bus master is giving up control of the bus and will switch its output lines to high impedance during the next bus cycle
27	RFU	Reserved for future use
28	RFU	Reserved for future use
29	A5	Address line 5

30	A4	Address line 4
31	A3	Address line 3
32	A15	Address line 15
33	A12	Address line 12
34	A9	Address line 9
35	DO1(M)/DATA1(M/S)	Data out line 1/bidirectional data line 1
36	DO0(M)/DATA0(M/S)	Data out line 0/bidirectional data line 0
37	A10(M)	Address line 10
38	DO4(M)/DATA4(M/S)	Data out line 4/bidirectional data line 4
39	DO5(M)/DATA5(M/S)	Data out line 5/bidirectional data line 5
40	DO6(M)/DATA6(M/S)	Data out line 6/bidirectional data line 6
41	DI2(M)/DATA10(M/S)	Data in line 2/bidirectional data line 10
42	DI3(M)/DATA11(M/S)	Data in line 3/bidirectional data line 11
43	DI7(M)/DATA15(M/S)	Data in line 7/bidirectional data line 15
44	s M1 (M)	M1 cycle. Status signal indicating op.-code fetch
45	s OUT (M)	Output. Status signal denoting data transfer to peripheral
46	s INP (M)	Input. Status signal denoting data transfer from a peripheral
47	s MEM R (M)	Memory read. Status signal denoting store read cycle
48	s HLTA (M)	Halt acknowledge. Status signal denoting execution of HLT instruction
49	CLOCK	A 2 MHz clock signal intended for timing operations; need not be synchronised to any other bus signals
50	EARTH	
51	+8 V	Unregulated supply for +5 V regulators
52	−16 V	Unregulated supply
53	EARTH	
54	$\overline{\text{SLAVE CLR}}$	Slave clear. Reset signal to bus slaves
55	$\overline{\text{DMA0}}$ (M)	DMA request line, lowest priority
56	$\overline{\text{DMA1}}$ (M)	DMA request line
57	$\overline{\text{DMA2}}$ (M)	DMA request line
58	s $\overline{\text{XTRQ}}$ (M)	Sixteen-bit request. Status signal from bus master requesting 16-bit data transfer
59	A19 (M)	Address line 19
60	$\overline{\text{SIXTN}}$ (S)	Sixteen acknowledge – response by slave to the master request s $\overline{\text{XTRQ}}$ if it can handle a 16-bit transfer. Open collector
61	A20	Extended address line 20
62	A21	Extended address line 21
63	A22	Extended address line 22
64	A23	Extended address line 23
65	NDEF	Not defined in standard
66	$\overline{\text{NDEF}}$	Not defined in standard
67	$\overline{\text{PHANTOM}}$ (M/S)	Phantom. Allows alternative set of bus slaves to share addresses with normal set. When asserted phantom slaves replace normal slaves

68	MWRT	Memory write strobe
69	RFU	Reserved for future use
70	EARTH	
71	RFU	Reserved for future use
72	RDY (S)	Ready. Indicates that slave is ready for data transfer. Open collector
73	$\overline{\text{INT}}$ (S)	Interrupt request. Normally maskable by program
74	$\overline{\text{HOLD}}$ (M)	Hold request. Temporary bus master requests control of bus. Open collector
75	$\overline{\text{RESET}}$	Reset. This sets bus master devices and is normally active at the same time as $\overline{\text{POC}}$ Open collector
76	p SYNC (M)	Sync. The control signal which indicates the initial bus state in a bus cycle
77	p $\overline{\text{WR}}$ (M)	Write. A strobe signal used to write data into a slave
78	p DBIN (M)	Data bus in. A strobe signal used to gate data from a slave to the data lines
79	A0	Address line 0. The least significant
80	A1	Address line 1
81	A2	Address line 2
82	A6	Address line 6
83	A7	Address line 7
84	A8	Address line 8
85	A13	Address line 13
86	A14	Address line 14
87	A11	Address line 11
88	DO2(M)/DATA2(M/S)	Data out line 2/bidirectional data line 2
89	DO3(M)/DATA3(M/S)	Data out line 3/bidirectional data line 3
90	DO7(M)/DATA7(M/S)	Data out line 7/bidirectional data line 7
91	DI4(M)/DATA12(M/S)	Data in line 4/bidirectional data line 12
92	DI5(M)/DATA13(M/S)	Data in line 5/bidirectional data line 13
93	DI6(M)/DATA14(M/S)	Data in line 6/bidirectional data line 14
94	DI1(M)/DATA9(M/S)	Data in line 1/bidirectional data line 9
95	DI0(M)/DATA8(M/S)	Data in line 0/bidirectional data line 8
96	s INTA (M)	Interrupt acknowledge
97	s $\overline{\text{WO}}$ (M)	Write output. A strobe signal used to gate data from a bus master to a slave
98	$\overline{\text{ERROR}}$ (S)	Error, indicating some error in a peripheral
99	$\overline{\text{POC}}$	Power on clear. Clears all devices attached to the bus when power is applied
100	EARTH	

$\overline{\text{NMI}}$ in which 1 or assertion denotes earth potential. The tag (M) indicates a signal which must be generated by the bus master. (S) indicates a signal which must be generated by a slave which uses the particular feature it controls. Thus not all slaves are required to generate all of the slave responses. In many situations some of the signals may be connected together, for example $\overline{\text{RESET}}$ and $\overline{\text{POC}}$.

7.3   The IEEE–488 or IEC 625 Bus

This bus has only 16 lines and was originally developed by Hewlett-Packard as a simple arrangement for connecting up to 15 instruments to a controller in order to take a set of readings and store or print out results. The controller was originally hard-wired, often with the ability to modify the procedure manually via switches or a plug board.

It met a growing need for compatibility between various measuring instruments and data-capturing devices, particularly in the field of automatic test equipment, and was widely accepted. Accordingly the IEEE decided that it formed the basis for a national standard, and it was then designated the IEEE–488 bus in place of the earlier title of GP–IB. It was also submitted for international recognition and a similar bus is now defined as the IEC 625 bus. This is electrically similar to the IEEE–488 bus but uses different connectors. The IEEE bus specified the original Hewlett-Packard 24-pin stackable connectors, but the IEC 625 standard specifies the same 25-way subminiature connectors as used for modems and other data-handling apparatus (V24 standard).

The IEC bus has eight bidirectional data lines, of which five are also used for addressing when the ATN line is energised. The bus protocol recognises three types of device which can be attached to the bus: listener, talker and controller. Only one controller can be attached to the bus, but there may be several talkers and listeners. Only one talker can be active at a time, but in contrast to other buses, several listeners may be active simultaneously. All signal levels are TTL-compatible, active low and the bus is terminated. The maximum length is 20 metres, with a maximum data rate of 2M bytes/s. Data are transmitted a byte at a time in parallel on the 8-bit data bus, but provision is made for asynchronous operation so that the slowest participant in a transfer can hold up the transaction until it is ready.

To avoid errors caused by devices outputting data simultaneously, all devices are allocated different addresses, and when any device is commanded to talk, all other talkers are automatically disabled.

The same process is not used for listening since several listeners are allowed to be active at the same time. Devices are called into operation by the commands TALK and LISTEN and turned off by the commands UNTALK and UNLISTEN.

Data transfer is controlled by three lines

DAV	—	Data valid
NRFD	—	Not ready for data
NDAC	—	Not data accepted

DAV is used by a talker to indicate that it has placed a byte of data on the data lines. The talker waits until the NDAC lines (wired-OR) goes high, signifying that all listeners that are active have accepted the data. It then ends the DAV signal, and waits for the NRFD line to go high. This is again a wired-OR, and will not respond until all listening devices have taken note of the data and are ready for the next byte.

The remaining five lines are concerned with bus management, and are as follows

ATN Attention. When this line is active, the information on the data lines is to be interpreted as a 7-bit command. Otherwise it is treated as an 8-bit byte of data.

IFC Interface clear. This puts all attached devices in a defined quiescent state, in the same manner as the power on reset.

SRQ Service request. This is asserted by a device and requests an interruption of the previous sequence of operations. It normally causes an interrupt and flag-testing sequence.

REN Remote enable. Many instruments attached to the bus have facilities for manual operation via front panel controls. This signal disables the manual controls and puts the instrument under the control of the bus.

EOI End or identify. This can be used in a multiple byte transfer to signal the last byte of the message. It can also be used by the controller, with the ATN line, to poll the bus devices.

Although the bus was originally designed for only 15 instruments, a secondary addressing feature has since been added which allows many more devices to be attached to the bus.

The 8-bit structure is very convenient for coupling to 8-bit microprocessors, and many systems now use microprocessors as the bus-controlling devices. In order to simplify the connection, several manufacturers provide interface packages designed to couple the IEC bus to the microprocessor bus. Examples of this are the Intel 8291 GPIB Talker/Listener, the Intel 8292 GPIB Controller, the Motorola MC68488 General Purpose Interface Adapter, and the Mullard HEF4738V. Also several complete microprocessor systems such as the Commodore PET provide an IEEE 488 bus for the connection of additional peripheral devices to the system.

The electrical specification of the bus, as revised by the IEEE, ensures that all devices which conform to the current standard will work correctly with one another, but no standard has been issued for data coding. Consequently a device attached to the bus may transmit in binary, BCD, ASCII or other code. Even in ASCII code there may be odd or even parity, or no parity. Thus the data format must be specified when procuring devices for the bus, or the controller must be able to undertake a variety of code conversions.

7.4　The E78 Europa Bus

Unlike the S−100 bus which was originally designed around the 8080 micro-processor, the E78 bus is not designed with any specific processor in mind. The two main considerations were to choose a general set of control signals which could adapt to any commonly used 8-bit processor, and to allow future 16-bit processors to be attached easily. The bus provides stabilised power supplies of ±5 V and ±12 V, 16 data lines and 16 address lines, with 4 extra address lines which can be used for 16-bit processors in place of 4 daisy chained interrupt lines. This allows the address space to be increased to 1M byte. There is a single DMA request and a DMA grant line, a standard and a nonmaskable inter-rupt line.

The board used with the E78 bus is the Double Eurocard, 160 mm X 233.4 mm, with a 64-way bus connector and another optional 64-way connector for external device lines. Signal levels are TTL-compatible, with negative logic (active low) using generally LS logic packages. To provide an adequate margin of safety the data and address lines should be driven to a new state at least 50 ns before the timing signal occurs, and they should be held for at least 50 ns after the timing signal has ended. The bus uses asynchronous protocol, with the controlling device asserting $\overline{\text{MREQ}}$ or $\overline{\text{IORQ}}$ and the slave replying with $\overline{\text{SLAK}}$ (slave acknowledge). When the master has asserted $\overline{\text{RD}}$ or $\overline{\text{WR}}$, the slave acknowledges the data transfer with $\overline{\text{TRAK}}$ (transfer acknowledge).

The main connector provides only the customary $\overline{\text{INT}}$ and $\overline{\text{NMI}}$ (non-maskable interrupt) lines but a further eight vectored interrupts $\overline{\text{INTV0}}$ to $\overline{\text{INTV7}}$ can be used on the second connector. The bus provides for devices other than the processor to acquire control of the bus, normally for DMA transfers, and bus request, bus available and bus busy lines are used to ensure orderly transfer of control and priority arbitration.

To avoid loading problems it is advised that each board should present no more than one LS TTL load, that is a capacitance of 16 pF, a current source of 50 μA or a current sink of 0.8 mA. $\overline{\text{INT}}$, $\overline{\text{NMI}}$, $\overline{\text{SLAK}}$ and $\overline{\text{TRAK}}$ can be driven by standard TTL open-collector gates such as the 7438, but the data bus, on account of its heavier loading, should be driven by tri-state or open-collector drivers which can sink a current of at least 24 mA.

7.5　The IEEE−796 Bus

This bus was designed by Intel for their first development system, called the Intellec, and adopted for subsequent development systems. It was called the Multibus, and as an increasing number of other manufacturers used it to build compatible plug-in boards for expanding Intel systems, the IEEE established a working group to draw up a standard based on the Multibus which would be acceptable nationally. Some changes from the original specification were made, for example the removal of a −5 V power line, but these were only minor ones. If needed, a −5 V supply can always be obtained from an on-board regulator since there is a −12 V line.

The bus uses an 86-way connector, with eight earth pins and eight +5 V pins to provide adequate current-handling capacity. The data bus has 16 bidirectional lines and there are 20 address lines and 8 interrupt request lines. All signal lines are TTL-compatible and are active low. The circuit boards used are 12 inches × 6.75 inches with a double-sided connector P1 for the bus, and an auxiliary connector P2 for external wiring. The boards plug directly into the edge connectors of the bus. Although originally used only for Intel microprocessor systems, this standard is now used by many other firms that make Intel-compatible boards for extending microprocessor systems.

7.6 Other Bus Standards

A number of other bus standards are currently in use, but they have not achieved the wide acceptance that the S−100 bus has obtained since they are nearly all designed for a specific type of microprocessor or system. The following list includes the more familiar ones, but is far from exhaustive.

(a)   The SS − 50/C bus

This was designed by the South West Technical Products Corporation for their 6800 microprocessor systems. It was closely specified and so did not suffer from the problems of incompatibility which arose with the looser specification of the original S−100 bus. In addition to the 6800 processor, the SS−50/C bus can easily be attached to the 6502 processor. The bus, being specific to the 6800, had originally 8 data lines and 16 address lines and the same set of control signals ($\overline{\text{VMA}}$, $\overline{\text{HALT}}$, $\overline{\text{NMI}}$, $\overline{\text{R/W}}$, $\overline{\text{RESET}}$, $\overline{\text{IRQ}}$) as the 6800. The power supplies are mixed; +8 V unregulated for on-board regulators with +5 V output, and ±12 V regulated. A unique feature is the inclusion of serial clocks from a crystal-controlled generator supplying bit rates of 110, 150, 300, 600 and 1200 bauds. Being intended only for an 8-bit processor the bus needs only 50 pins in all. The connectors used are single-sided with pin 33 cut away to provide an index. This prevents the board from being inserted the wrong way round. Boards which contain peripheral packages need only decode a few address lines, and to reduce board costs a 30-way board (SS−30 peripheral card) can be used which does not include address lines. The decoding is performed on another board and only chip select and register select lines are taken to the SS−30 board.

When the M6809 processor was introduced some changes were made to the pin allocations of the original SS−50 bus, and the current version, designated

SS—50/C has provision for 20 address lines, a fast interrupt request line and a few extra control signals. These are obtained by using two lines which were originally undefined, and eliminating the 5-bit rate clock signals. Also the ±12 V lines have been changed to ±16 V unregulated supplies, so that all supplies need on-board regulators, as does the S—100 bus.

(b)   The PET Bus

The Commodore PET microcomputer has an IEEE port and also has most of the processor bus lines brought out to an edge connector on the side of the case. This is a double-sided 80-wire device, in which all odd-numbered pins are earthed and are located on the top side of the connector. The signals available are 12 address lines (A0—A11), 8 data lines, R/W, Ø2, $\overline{\text{RESET}}$, $\overline{\text{IRQ}}$ and 11 select lines. The latter are decoded outputs of the higher-order address lines and select 4K byte blocks of the address space. Select line 1 is energised by addresses between 1000 and 1FFF (hexadecimal), select line 2 by addresses between 2000 and 2FFF, etc. This double provision allows the user to add extra peripheral devices very easily via the IEEE bus, and also to add large blocks of storage which need access to a correspondingly large address space via the PET bus.

(c)   The Exorciser Bus

This was introduced by Motorola for their M6800 development systems. It is based upon an 86-way double-sided printed circuit connector, and includes all of the address, data and control lines of the M6800 microprocessor together with some additional lines for slow store packages (MEM RDY), a store clock (MEM CLK), a store refresh clock ($\overline{\text{REF}}$ $\overline{\text{CLK}}$), refresh request ($\overline{\text{REF}}$ $\overline{\text{REQ}}$) and refresh grant ($\overline{\text{REF}}$ $\overline{\text{GNT}}$). The latter two are for use with dynamic data storage packages. Stabilised supplies of ±5 V and ±12 V are provided, and there are 24 spare lines as yet undefined.

(d)   The LSI—11 Bus

The LSI—11 is a microprocessor member of the Digital Equipment Corporation's 16-bit PDP—11 family of minicomputers. It is program-compatible with the PDP—11 but the bus arrangements are somewhat different, because the LSI—11 has a multiplexed data/address bus, whereas the PDP—11 has separate data and address lines. Physically the LSI—11 bus uses sockets which mate with two double-sided printed circuit edge connectors, giving 72 lines in all. The main power line is +5 V, with auxiliary supplies of ±12 V. The same asynchronous handshaking protocol is used for data transfers between a bus master and a slave, with provision for daisy-chained DMA request and DMA grant signals. Further lines provide for refreshing dynamic storage and for providing a +5 V back-up supply to retain data in RAM when the main power supply has been turned off.

The final section of the chapter is devoted to serial data transmission. Although not concerned with microprocessor bus arrangements, it is convenient to include standards for these with the standards discussed above for parallel data transfer.

7.7 Serial Data Standards

Although parallel data transfer is simple and fast, it inevitably calls for many lines between the computer and the data device. Unless the two are fairly close, the cable cost becomes prohibitive, and serial transmission along a single pair of wires is preferred. An early standard for the electrical signals was devised to suit the teleprinters almost invariably attached to early minicomputers. This was called the 20 mA current loop interface. In this the computer output information to the printing mechanism was coded as mark condition = logic 1 = current of 20 mA, space condition = logic 0 = no current flowing. Data in the other direction came from the transmitting contacts of the keyboard which were closed for a mark and open for a space. The computer interface provided a current source to energise the contacts and a voltage-sensing circuit to detect whether the contacts were open or closed.

This arrangement was convenient in that the teleprinter was passive and needed no power supply for the interface signals, but it was awkward in that the two halves were asymmetrical. Thus two teleprinters could not be connected together to check one another, and similarly for two computer interfaces.

A widely used standard for similar purposes originated from the International Telecommunications Union, whose telegraph and telephone committee (CCITT) proposed the V24 and V28 standards for connecting data-handling equipment to modems. These standards define both a set of signal levels and line impedances, and a set of signalling lines and their functional meaning. The standard which defines the electrical interface between the data-transmission equipment and the modem is V24; this has also been adopted widely for connecting teleprinters, VDUs, and data terminals to computers. Almost all microprocessors with a serial data interface will meet the V24 specification.

The signals are defined as follows:

Mark = logic 1 = -3 V to -15 V, nominally -6 V
Space = logic 0 = $+3$ V to $+15$ V, nominally $+6$ V

The maximum open-circuit voltage on any line must not exceed ± 25 V to earth, and the maximum short-circuit current between any two lines must not exceed 500 mA. The impedance presented to the transmitter must have a resistive component between 3 kΩ and 7 kΩ, with a parallel capacitance not exceeding 2500 pF.

The standard was intended for short cable runs of 50 feet or less, since the line cannot be correctly terminated, but at slow data rates up to 600 or 1200 bauds it can be used over much longer distances of 1000 feet or more. For short runs the maximum data rate specified is 20 000 bauds.

Most V24 circuits are operated in duplex mode, which involves simultaneous transmission and reception. This requires a 3-wire circuit, consisting of a transmit line, a receive line and a common earth.

Since the V24 interface is symmetrical with regard to circuit conditions (active transmitter, passive receiver, both using the same signal levels) any device to V24 standards can be connected to any other such device and will be electrically compatible. It can of course only exchange data correctly if both devices use the same bit rate and character code. Also any duplex circuit can be looped (send and receive lines connected together) to test the circuit. This is a valuable feature when fault finding.

The V24 signal levels are now used so widely that integrated circuits are available which convert from TTL levels to V24, and also in the reverse direction.

A virtually identical standard is known in the USA as RS–232–C. Like the V24 interface, it specifies the use of a 25-way subminiature D-type connector, and allocates particular pins for the various signals involved.

Although the V24 standard can handle any data rate which can be modulated on to a telephone circuit (typical bandwidth 300–3400 Hz), it is unable to cope with the much greater data rates of computer to computer, or computer to fast terminal links. For this application, two other standards were developed, RS–423 and RS–422. These enable signal reflections at impedance changes in the circuit to be reduced considerably, since the line terminating resistor can be reduced to 450 Ω minimum (RS–423) or to 100 Ω (RS–422). By choosing a line which has a characteristic impedance of 450 Ω or more, RS–423 enables a correct termination to be used, so minimising ringing and reflections, and enabling a much greater data rate to be transmitted without errors. For RS–422 a closely spaced twisted pair can be used with a characteristic impedance near to 100 Ω.

A difficulty with V24 circuits is that an unbalanced line with earth return is used, and the earth return must be connected to the local earth at each end. Consequently the circuits can suffer from common-mode interference, due to the potential difference between the two earths. To minimise this, RS–232 was originally specified for a maximum length of 50 feet, which is much too short a run for many applications. Historically the common-mode noise problem was diminished by increasing the signal level to ±80 V, but this large signal swing is suitable only for the slowest circuits, and does not easily couple to transistor drivers and receivers. By allowing the transmission line to be terminated correctly, RS–423 enabled data rates to be increased to 100K bauds, and the maximum cable length to be increased to 4000 feet, still using unbalanced lines.

By changing to balanced lines with differential drivers and receivers, RS–422 enables the data rate to be increased to 10M bauds with the same maximum cable length.

A further change from the V24 interface is that RS–422 and RS–423 allow one driver and up to ten receivers to be connected to the line, whereas V24 permits only one driver and one receiver. A future standard based on RS–422 will allow up to 32 driver/receiver pairs to be connected to the line, which is correctly terminated at each end. The line then becomes a data bus but, unlike the previous computer buses described in earlier sections, it is operated in a serial rather than parallel mode, and it is electrically balanced, whereas all other buses use unbalanced signals with a common earth return.

8 System Testing and Development

8.1 System Development

It is unrealistic to assume when designing microprocessor systems that programs and interface connections can be developed on paper and will then always perform as intended. Almost invariably there will be initial errors which can be discovered only by running the system and monitoring its behaviour. This is particularly the case with programs for high-volume products which are held in mask ROM. The mask charge may be several thousand pounds, and the slightest error will require a new mask and another charge for designing and making it.

For this reason microprocessor manufacturers produce development systems. These in their simplest form allow the user to load a program from a keyboard, run it either at full speed or an instruction at a time, and pause at any stage to examine the contents of the main processor registers. To avoid having to traverse a loop many times manually, breakpoints may be inserted into the program. The processor can then run at full speed until it reaches the breakpoint, where it halts. The program can then be operated an instruction at a time and its action can be checked. Since the program is held in RAM, any instruction can be changed and the process repeated.

When the program has been run successfully, it can be output through a serial interface to a cassette tape recorder so that a permanent copy is available. Playback from the recorder allows the program to be fed back into the computer on a subsequent occasion. Normally when the power is removed from the development system the contents of the RAM disappear. Larger systems can have floppy discs attached for program storage.

In order to enable a keyboard and display to be used in this manner, a small ROM is fitted, typically 1K bytes, containing a monitor program, and one or two I/O packages to allow external devices to be attached.

The smaller systems consist of one or two boards, but for larger applications multiple board systems are available, such as the Intel 'Intellec' and the Motorola 'Exorciser'. These have a processor board and power supply as a minimum system and can be extended by inserting extra boards containing I/O packages, extra storage, a floppy-disc controller, or a PROM programmer. For high-volume applications a paper tape containing the program is generally required, for generating the mask ROM. For this output a paper-tape punch can be attached to a serial output channel.

A small development system will accept only hexadecimal input in machine code form, but larger systems with a floppy-disc store and adequate RAM have room for an assembler program stored on the disc, so enabling the programmer to operate in assembly language. In some cases a high-level language such as Pascal may be available, so easing the programming task.

Another useful facility is the ability to transfer a developed program to an EPROM for building into a prototype system.

For program development there may be some advantage in using an existing minicomputer or main-frame machine with its large file-storage features, editor, etc. For this a cross-assembler program is needed. This accepts the assembly language of the microprocessor as input, but outputs machine code in the microprocessor format rather than that of the host machine.

8.2   ROM Simulators

Before committing a program to an expensive mask-fabrication process it can be tested by building a prototype system with a separate program store. In place of the normal program ROM, a ROM simulator can be used. This consists of a writable store, with facilities for loading, checking and amending the contents, which can be switched to read-only mode. The connections are terminated on a plug which is inserted into the socket which normally contains the program ROM. The system can then be tested with all the peripherals and I/O packages of the working system and the program can easily be amended if necessary. Some elaborate development systems provide cross-assemblers and other software aids, and also enable the machine code version of the program to be held in a ROM simulator, so that it can easily be amended during the program-testing phase.

8.3   Board Testing

The first stage in testing a complete microprocessor system is to check that the printed circuit wiring contains no short-circuits or open-circuits. This is straightforward if the major packages are mounted in sockets, and can be re-placed by test plugs. Where the packages are soldered in place, a test clip can be fitted which connects a wire to each pin, but the tri-state control and chip enable pins must be connected to a test point so that the line drivers can all be disabled. Only then can the bus wiring be tested adequately. Usually each line is tested to ensure that it can be driven to earth, +5 V, and can also float at an intermediate voltage.

Having checked that the wiring is correct, peripheral packages can be tested by setting up their addresses on the address bus and the appropriate control signals on the control lines. Where these are applied externally, there may be a need to disable the internal clock and provide an external clock supply synchronised with the other timing and control signals.

An alternative method of providing test signals is to use the system microprocessor to generate them from a program held in the normal program ROM, or held in a separate ROM which can be plugged into a spare socket on the board.

8.4   In-circuit Emulators

Another method of testing the final version of a microprocessor system is to allow the user control over the action of the microprocessor package itself. This requires the processor to be mounted in a socket.

The processor is removed and replaced by a plug connected to a system usually based upon the same microprocessor package called an in-circuit emulator. This has facilities for monitoring the action of the processor, halting it when a particular event occurs, examining its register contents, etc. Data storage is included in the more comprehensive systems, so that when a halt occurs a trace is available of the last 100 or so bytes which have been sent to the data or address bus. There may also be facilities for recording the flow of data to or from the I/O packages. Also the data stream may be scanned for the appearance of either a particular address or data word, and the processor can be halted to enable the registers and other information to be examined. In some systems the processor can be controlled either by the normal ROM, or by a copy of the program held in the in-circuit emulator RAM. With the latter, any instruction can be changed to investigate its effect on the task performed.

One practical difficulty with emulators is that the simplest types cater for only one model of microprocessor. Thus a separate emulator is needed for each type of microprocessor used. As an alternative several instrument manufacturers have produced 'universal' emulators which can deal with several types of microprocessor. However, for each type, the user must buy a 'personality card' containing special logic to generate the correct bus timing and control signals, and often a floppy disc or cassette holding the program needed to control the emulator hardware. This makes a universal emulator which can cope with, say, four types of microprocessor an expensive instrument.

Most in-circuit emulators allow the user to insert breakpoints in the program, execute single instructions under manual control ('single shot'), or start executing at full speed from any part of the program.

Since most programs initially contain errors, users are generally advised to check programs a section at a time, so reducing the area to be searched for a fault and enabling it to be found and corrected easily. Also, simple test programs can be run to check the behaviour of the peripheral devices, so making it easier to identify whether faults arise from hardware or software.

8.5 Logic State Analysers

Although the oscilloscope is the major fault-finding tool for investigating hard-wired logic systems, it is less valuable when applied to microprocessor systems. Whereas conventional logic can be given a repeated set of input signals, so that the oscilloscope has a cyclic signal to which it can synchronise, a microprocessor running a typical program has no such cyclic pattern. Consequently, there is no fixed signal pattern to which the oscilloscope can be locked, apart from short program loops, which may only be executed for a brief period. Also a single data channel is rarely sufficient to locate errors. In order to trace the sequence of program execution it is necessary to record the succession of addresses from which successive instructions are fetched; this requires the recording of 16 address bits simultaneously for each instruction.

In order to provide a comprehensive fault-finding instrument it is necessary to abandon the principle of the simple oscilloscope, that is, that data are displayed as they occur, and provide the means for recording a burst of 4K bytes or more of data. The user can then select how these data are to be displayed, and run through them sequentially.

The data are normally captured by attaching probes to the bus lines, or a clip which contacts all pins of the microprocessor. The following inputs are normally required

(1) Signal inputs. These are generally either from the address bus or the data bus. There may be 8, 16, 24 or 32 bits captured simultaneously. Some instruments allow a variable logic threshold to be used when sampling these inputs, otherwise the threshold may be switched to standard values for TTL or MOS logic.
(2) Clock inputs, normally one or two signals from the system under test. The analyser can be set to trigger on either the rising or the falling edge of the clock pulse.
(3) Clock qualifiers. These are additional signals which indicate particular actions or processor states, such as $\overline{WR}$, $\overline{RD}$, $\overline{MEMRQ}$, $\overline{IORQ}$, etc. These may be up to six lines, generally logically ANDed together. The particular combination used may be determined by physically connecting probes, or by keyboard input which enables each qualifier signal to be treated as either an essential input or a 'don't care'. Also each probe input can be read using either positive or negative logic convention.

For some purposes other signals such as VMA may be used either as a qualifier or as a clock signal.

Where the action of a particular package is concerned, its chip enable signal can be used as a clock input, so recording all transfers to or from the package and disregarding others.

For many 8-bit microprocessors the signal probes are divided into a 16-bit group to sense the address lines and an 8-bit group to sense the data lines. A trigger signal can be derived from either group by setting in a particular address or data word. A trigger signal occurs when the bus signals are identical to the word previously entered. Thereafter signals are sampled either at each clock pulse, or at each subsequent trigger event. In order to analyse many faults it is necessary to examine processor activity before the fault occurred. For this purpose the trigger can be arranged to stop the recording of data rather than to start it. Then if the analyser has a capacity for storing say 250 samples, these will be the 250 samples leading up to the trigger event. For greater flexibility most analysers include a counter, so that the start of sampling can be delayed until a prescribed number of clock cycles or trigger events has occurred. This allows a range of processor activity relative to the trigger event to be recorded and analysed.

The data recorded can be presented in a variety of ways, the simplest being binary format. This is lengthy and difficult to check, so most analysers make provision for displaying results also in octal or hexadecimal format. A more elaborate provision is made in some microprocessor-controlled analysers whereby a reverse assembler or disassembler is incorporated. Then when program instructions are being sampled, they can be displayed in mnemonic form as well as in hexadecimal notation. This of course requires storage of the instruction set of each microprocessor likely to be used, and thus becomes expensive if more than one or two types are handled.

A final mode sometimes available is that of a timing diagram, where each line sampled produces a graph of signal level against time similar to a conventional multichannel oscilloscope.

8.6 Asynchronous Display

All the previous description relates to synchronous sampling in which the analyser records are sampled only for each processor clock pulse. This gives sufficient data to track down a program error, but cannot detect a spurious pulse or 'glitch' which might for example cause a false interrupt.

In order to detect these, and other failures due to timing errors within a clock interval, some analysers with fast logic can be operated asynchronously. In this mode the sampling of data is controlled by a much faster clock within the analyser, operating at typically 10–20 MHz. The microprocessor remains under the control of its own clock supply, typically 1–2 MHz, not synchronised to the analyser clock. Thus ten or more samples of each probe signal can be recorded within each microprocessor clock cycle. By using circuits which stretch very short transients to, say 60 ns pulses, one can ensure that a probe which is sampled at least every 50 ns (a 20 MHz clock rate) will detect the presence of the transient.

Operating in this manner, 250 data samples will correspond to only 25–50 clock cycles of the microprocessor. This is however a restriction which can be accepted in return for the fine detail of signal timing which it reveals.

A particularly difficult fault to trace is one which occurs only rarely, when some particular data pattern or event sequence occurs. The logic analyser can be very useful for investigating these faults by arranging that data are stored continuously and the only action which causes a trigger event arises from the fault condition. The trigger is then switched to end data storage, and the system is left running. When a fault occurs, the analyser will contain say 250 data samples preceding the fault, and by sampling various sets of signals the trouble can usually be identified. This method of using the analyser is often called the 'baby-sitting' mode.

8.7   Graphical Displays

A relatively cheap and useful method of checking the path that a processor follows through the program is to plot its trajectory on an oscilloscope. The address of each instruction is sampled when it appears on the address bus during the instruction fetch cycle. The upper and lower bytes are stored in D-type bistables whose outputs feed two 8-bit DACs. These in turn feed the X and Y amplifiers of an oscilloscope. Thus each different address in the address space will cause the spot to be deflected to a particular point on the screen. Most microprocessor action involves the processor being held in loops of instructions for varying intervals, and these will produce bright traces of closed figures on the screen. Program segments traversed once or only occasionally will be less bright.

This kind of display is most convenient for comparison puposes, when the various patterns produced by a system under test can be compared with the patterns produced by a system known to work correctly.

An alternative but less discriminating display can be obtained by taking all 16 address bits to a DAC feeding the Y amplifiers and driving the X plates from a conventional time base. This arrangement does however give adequate resolution for examining 8-bit data signals.

8.8   Signature Analysis

Microprocessors and their associated LSI packages have very many possible logical states, and testing for only a few of these generates vast amounts of data. In order to simplify the detection of correct and incorrect operation, some method of data compression is almost essential. This reduces the amount of information that must be scanned to manageable proportions. One widely used scheme is the generation of a cyclic redundancy check character. This operates on a continuous stream of bits which is passed through a shift register. A modulo-2 adder precedes the input to the shift register and in addition to the incoming bit stream it is also fed with several feedback signals from various stages of the shift register. In order to obtain the greatest certainty of error detection, the last tap is taken from the last stage of the shift register, as shown in figure 8.1. The shift register is initially cleared and then a stream of bits is sent to it. Typically a 16-bit register is used, and the bit pattern left after accepting the data is called its 'signature'. This is usually read as four hexadecimal characters. Each bit sequence produces its particular signature, and if any single bit is changed the signature also changes. Thus there is the certainty of detecting single bit errors and a very high probability of detecting multiple errors.

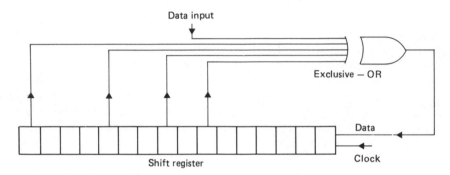

Figure 8.1 Logic for signature analysis

Signature analysis is usually applied by generating a known sequence of input data, and measuring the signature at various points along the data path for a system known to be working correctly. To trace a fault to a particular section of the system, the operator searches for a unit which has correct signatures at its inputs, but a faulty signature at its output.

Signature analysis is a general technique which has been applied to a range of digital systems, but it has particular advantages for testing microprocessor systems. Some extra program can be held in the ROM which will generate a test sequence for measuring signatures. Input/output operations can be checked by transferring a known sequence of data and measuring the signature at various ports. For example an input port and an output port can be checked by using a short program which reads data presented to the input port and echoes them back at the output port. The data stream is supplied to the input port and the signature measured at the output port.

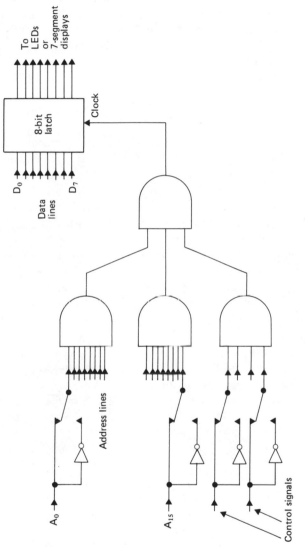

Figure 8.2 Universal port

ROMs can be checked by reading all of their stored data and evaluating the signature. This may be stored for reference in the ROM itself.

For the tests mentioned above, the processor will be driven from its own clock and the signature analyser will be synchronised with it. For other tests the analyser may need its own clock which will also drive the system under test.

Although the signature analyser has been described as a separate instrument, some comprehensive logic analysers can also be switched to operate in a signature analysis mode.

8.9   Other Fault-finding Aids

For the rapid and effective tracing of errors, logic analysers and in-circuit emulators offer unrivalled assistance. However, they are expensive instruments and simpler apparatus can often provide useful information more cheaply. An example of this is the graphical display of bus addresses using two D/A converters and a laboratory oscilloscope. Another is the universal port. This is an 8-bit set of D-type bistables which is attached to the data lines. It has full 16-bit address decoding, each address line having a switch so that the gate input can be connected either to the address line directly, or through an inverter. The output of the address-selecting gate is used as a clock for the bistables. This enables any address to be selected, and whenever this occurs the corresponding data will be stored in the bistables. In addition to the address signal, it is useful to have facilities for gating in control signals such as $\overline{RO}$, $\overline{WR}$, $\overline{MEMRQ}$, $\overline{IORQ}$, etc. as shown in figure 8.2.

The arrangement can be elaborated by adding a small store which can be loaded continuously from the system. Then when the processor is stopped, this store contains the last, say 30 bytes which were transferred to or from the address. These can be read out manually and displayed on 7-segment LEDs.

9 Interfacing to 16 - Bit Microprocessors

9.1 16-Bit Bus Organisation

In the last few years several 16-bit microprocessors have become available. These were initially used only for special applications where both rapid calculations and high accuracy were called for, for example in critical control systems. As prices fell with increased production they were used in other areas, but they currently represent only a few per cent of the total microprocessor market.

The interface facilities for these processors are very similar to those for 8-bit devices; since many peripherals, particularly those involved in communications, are byte-wide devices, the same peripheral packages can be used on both 8-bit and 16-bit processors. One difference between the two types is that, to minimise the number of pins on the processor package, most 16-bit processors have multiplexed data and address lines. The 8-bit processors either have separate address and data buses (M6800, Z80, 8080, etc.) or multiplex the data lines and the lower 8 address lines (8085, etc.).

Thus some storage of the address information is required when connecting Z80 and 8080 peripheral packages to a multiplexed 16-bit address/data bus. The simplest packages to connect are those designed for a multiplexed bus such as is used on the 8085.

9.2 The Intel 8086 Family

The Intel 8086 was one of the first 16-bit microprocessors to be produced in quantity. It has an ALE output (address latch enable) which provides a timing pulse to latch the address information from the common address/data bus. This functions in exactly the same manner as the ALE output on the 8085 processor. All of the storage packages designed for the 8085 (8155, 8355, 8755) have an address latch on the chip, so no additional logic is needed for the address lines.

The 8086 was originally intended to use the 8085 and 8080 series of interface packages, supplemented by a few special interfaces intended to exploit the greater capacity of the 16-bit processor. The following list shows the wide range of peripheral packages which can be attached to either 8-bit or 16-bit microprocessors.

8085 Family Interface Packages

8155	Static RAM + I/O Ports + Timer
8355	ROM + I/O Ports
8755	EPROM + I/O Ports
8251	Programmable Communications Interface
8253	Programmable Interval Timer
8255	Programmable Peripheral Interface
8257	Programmable DMA Controller
8275	Programmable CRT Controller
8279	Programmable Keyboard/Display Interface
8291	IEEE—488 Talker/Listener
8292	IEEE—488 Controller
8293	IEEE—488 Transceiver

Packages designed specifically for the 8086 include

8284   Clock Generator and Driver.

8289   Bus Arbiter. This arbitrates between the various requests for bus control in a multi-processor system.

8237   Programmable DMA Controller. This provides for four DMA channels, providing storage for addresses, a word count, and arbitrating between the channel requests for DMA transfer.

8259   Programmable Interrupt Controller. This accepts 8 inputs (expandable to 64) and selects that having the highest priority when multiple interrupts are requested.

In order to enable the full transfer rate of the 8086 to be used, a micro-processor-based I/O processor, the 8089, can be added to the bus. This acts as an intelligent DMA controller, and has two I/O channels which can handle transfer rates up to 1.25M bytes/s with the standard clock rate of 5 MHz. It supports any combination of 8-bit and 16-bit buses, and has a limited instruction set designed for I/O transactions. It shares the program storage with the main 8086 processor.

Since so many peripheral devices require 8-bit transfers, Intel have produced the 8088, which has the same instruction set and internal data bus as the 8086. Externally however, it has only an 8-bit bus and is compatible with 8080 and 8085 peripheral packages.

9.3   The Motorola M68000

The Motorola M68000 is a powerful 16-bit processor which contains 32-bit internal registers, and can directly address 16M bytes of storage. It is unusual in that no attempt was made to limit the number of pins to the 40 used for most 8-bit processors. By deciding on a 64-pin package the designer has provided separate address and data lines, so simplifying and speeding up I/O and store transfers. The control signals were specifically intended to allow the standard M6800 peripheral packages to be connected directly to the bus, for example

6821	Peripheral Interface Adapter
6840	Programmable Timer Module
6845	CRT Controller
6850	Asynchronous Communications Interface Adapter
6852	Synchronous Serial Data Adapter
68488	IEEE–488 Interface Adapter

Several interface packages have also been introduced which take advantage of the 16-bit bus structure of the M68000, such as

68230	Parallel Interface/Timer
68450	DMA Controller
68560	Serial DMA Controller
68561	Multi-Protocol Communications Controller

Where the full power of the 68000 is not required, a program-compatible version having an 8-bit external bus, the 68008, can be used. This can accept all of the 6800-family peripheral packages and needs only 8-bit storage, so reducing system costs considerably. An upwards-compatible version of the family, the 68020, is planned for 1983 which will support virtual storage and has a 32-bit external bus.

Second source agreements have been made with Signetics and Mostek which will bring other peripheral packages to the market. For example, Signetics are currently developing the following

SC 68681	Dual Universal Asynchronous Receiver/Transmitter
SC 68562	Dual Universal Serial Communications Controller
SC 68430	Direct Memory Access Interface
SC 68454	Intelligent Multiple Disc Controller
SC 68459	Disc Phase-Locked Loop

Mostek have announced a 16-bit microcomputer (MK 68200) which has on-chip storage, timers and a range of I/O functions optimised for control applications. Other package include

MK 68564	Serial I/O Controller
MK 68901	Multifunction Peripheral
MK 68590	Local Area Network Controller for Ethernet

9.4   The Zilog Z8000

The Z8000 family processors use multiplexed 16-bit data/address lines and have sixteen 16-bit internal registers with provision for addressing them as 8-bit, 16-bit, 32-bit or 64-bit registers. The Z8002 can directly address 64K bytes and is a 40-pin device; the Z8001 has seven extra segment address lines, can address a total of 8M bytes and is a 48-pin device.

The I/O instructions provide for 8-bit or 16-bit transfers, and include a 16-bit port address. This uses the address lines but does not inpinge upon the store address space, since it has a separate I/O address space.

Peripherals and storage are connected to Z8000 family processors via the Z-bus which is a fast parallel shared bus which multiplexes data and address information and comprises the following signals (O denotes CPU output, I denotes CPU input)

(a) Primary signals (timing, control and data transfer)

AD0–AD15   Multiplexed address/data lines.

EXTENDED ADDRESS (O) These comprise the higher-order address lines; their number depends on the CPU configuration and the amount of storage

ST0–ST3 STATUS (O)   These indicate the type of action that the CPU is engaged upon

$\overline{\text{AS}}$ (O) ADDRESS STROBE. The rising edge denotes the beginning of a transaction and that the address, status R/$\overline{\text{W}}$ and B/$\overline{\text{W}}$ signals are valid

$\overline{\text{DS}}$ (O)   DATA STROBE. Provides the timing signals for data transfer

R/$\overline{\text{W}}$ (O) READ/WRITE. Read = high level; Write = low level. Denotes the direction of a data transfer

B/$\overline{\text{W}}$ (O)   Byte/Word. Byte = high; Word = low. Indicates whether a byte or a 16-bit word of data is to be transferred along a 16-bit bus

$\overline{\text{WAIT}}$ (I)   Used by a slow peripheral to hold up processor action until its own cycle has been completed

$\overline{\text{RESET}}$ (I) Used for initial start-up

Also each package is provided with a $\overline{\text{CS}}$ (chip select) signal, gated from the address and status lines.

(b) Bus request signals (for bus control)

$\overline{\text{BUSREQ}}$ Asserted by a device requesting control of the bus

$\overline{\text{BUSACK}}$ (O)   Generated by the processor to indicate that it has relinquished control of the bus

$\overline{\text{BAI}}$ Bus acknowledge in ⎫

⎬ signals in the bus-request daisy-chain connection

$\overline{\text{BAO}}$ Bus acknowledge out ⎭

(c) Interrupt signals

INT (I)   Generated by a peripheral requesting an interrupt

INTACK   Interrupt acknowledge. This signal is decoded from the status lines

IEI, IEO   Interrupt enable in; interrupt enable out. These signals form the interrupt daisy-chain connection

There are also four signals which can be used for requesting a shared resource and allocating it in a multiple-microprocessor system.

Peripheral packages designed for the Z8000 family include

Z8016   DMA Controller, a fast dual-channel device

Z8030   Serial Communication Controller, a dual-channel multi-protocol component

Z8036   Counter and Parallel I/O. This has three 16-bit counter/timers, 3 I/O Ports

Z8034   Universal Peripheral Controller, containing an 8-bit CPU, 3 I/O ports and program storage

Z8038   FIO Input/Output Interface Unit. This has a first-in, first-out data buffer which can store 128 bytes of data, two 7-bit registers and control/status registers

Z8052   CRT Controller

In addition the Z80 peripheral packages can be interfaced with a little extra logic to the Z-bus.

Bibliography

(1)   Microprocessor Architecture and Applications

Aspinall, D. (Ed.) *The Microprocessor and Its Application*. Cambridge University Press, Cambridge, 1978

Bennett, W. S. and Evert, C. F. *What Every Engineer Should Know About Microcomputers*. M. Dekker, New York, 1980

Boyce, J. C. *Microprocessor and Microcomputer Basics*. Prentice-Hall International, Hemel Hempstead, 1979

Burton, D. P. and Dexter, A. C. *Microprocessor System Handbook*. Analog Devices, Norwood, Massachusetts, 1977

Garland, H. *Introduction to Microprocessor System Design*. McGraw-Hill, New York, 1979

Gibson, G. A. and Lin, Y-C. *Microcomputers for Engineers and Scientists*. Prentice-Hall International, Hemel Hempstead, 1981

Greenfield, S. E. *Architecture of Microprocessors*. Prentice-Hall, Englewood Cliffs, New Jersey, 1979

Heffer, D. E., King G. A. and Keith, G. *Basic Principles and Practice of Microprocessors*. Edward Arnold, London, 1981

Heiserman, D. C. *Handbook of Digital I. C. Applications*. Prentice-Hall International, Hemel Hempstead, 1980

Huggins, E. *Microprocessors and Microcomputers: Their use and programming*. Macmillan Press, London, 1979

Katz, P. *Digital Control using Microprocessors*. Prentice-Hall International, Hemel Hempstead, 1981

Lenk, J. D. *Handbook of Microprocessors, Microcomputers and Minicomputers*. Prentice-Hall International, Hemel Hempstead, 1979

Lesea, A. and Zaks, R. *Microprocessor Interfacing Techniques*. SYBEX, Berkeley, California, 1977

Leventhal, L. A. *Introduction to Microprocessors*. Prentice-Hall, Englewood Cliffs, New Jersey, 1978

Morris, N. M. *Microprocessor and Microcomputer Technology*. Macmillan Press, London, 1981

Osborne, A. *Introduction to Microcomputing*, Volumes 0–3. Osborne and Associates, Berkeley, California, 1977

Pashow, E. J. (Ed.) *Microcomputer Interfacing*. McGraw-Hill, New York, 1981

Peatman, J. B. *Microcomputer-based Design*. McGraw-Hill, New York, 1977

Poe, E. C. and Goodwin, J. C. *The S−100 and Other Micro Buses.* Howard W. Sams, Indianapolis, 1981
Roberts S. K. *Industrial Design and Microcomputers.* Prentice-Hall International, Hemel Hempstead, 1982
Titus, C. A. *et al. 16-bit Microprocessors.* Prentice-Hall, Englewood Cliffs, New Jersey, 1981
Walker, B. S. *Understanding Microprocessors.* Macmillan Press, London, 1982
Witten, I. H. *Communicating with Microprocessors.* Academic Press, London, 1980

(2)   Books on Particular Types of Microprocessor

Barden, W. *The Z-80 Microcomputer Handbook.* Howard W. Sams, Indianapolis, 1979
Bishop, R. *Basic Microprocessors and the 6800.* Hayden Book Co., Rochelle Park, New Jersey, 1979
Fawcett, B. K. *The Z-8000 Microprocessor: A Design Handbook.* Prentice-Hall International, Hemel Hempstead, 1982
Greenfield, J. D. and Wray, W. C. *Using Microprocessors and Microcomputers: The 6800 family.* John Wiley, Chichester, 1981
De Jong, M. L. *Programming and Interfacing the 6502, with Experiments.* Prentice-Hall International, Hemel Hempstead, 1980
Leventhal, L. A. *Microcomputer Experimentation with the Motorola MEK 6800 D2.* Prentice-Hall International, Hemel Hempstead, 1981
Morse, S. P. *The 8086 Primer.* Hayden Book Co., Rochelle Park, New Jersey, 1978
Nicols, J. C., Nichols, E. A. and Rony, P. R. *Z-80 Microprocessor Programming and Interfacing* (2 Volumes). Howard W. Sams, Indianapolis, 1979
Poe, E. *Using the 6800 Microprocessor.* Howard W. Sams, Indianapolis, 1978
Rony, P. *8080A Microcomputer Interfacing and Programming.* Prentice-Hall International, Hemel Hempstead, 1982
Scanlon, L. J. *The 6800: Principles and Programming.* Prentice-Hall International, Hemel Hempstead, 1981
Staugaard, A. C. Jr. *How to Program and Interface the 6800.* Prentice-Hall International, Hemel Hempstead, 1981
Staugaard, A. C. Jr. *6801, 68701 and 6803 Microcomputer Programming and Interfacing.* Prentice-Hall International, Hemel Hempstead, 1981
Staugaard, A. C. Jr. *6809 Microcomputer Programming and Interfacing.* Prentice-Hall International, Hemel Hempstead, 1981
Williamson, I. and Dale, R. *Understanding Microprocessors with the MK14.* Macmillan Press, London, 1980

(3) Transducers, D/A and A/D Converters

Benedict, R. P. *Fundamentals of Temperature, Pressure and Flow Measurements.*
2nd Edition. John Wiley, London, 1977

Clayton, G. B. *Data Converters.* Macmillan Press, London, 1982

Garrett, P. H. *Analog Systems for Microprocessors and Minicomputers.* Prentice-
Hall International, Hemel Hempstead, 1978

Sydenham, P. H. *Transducers in Measurement and Control.* Adam Hilger, Bristol,
1980

Titus, J. A. *et al. Microcomputer—Analog Converter Software and Hardware
Interfacing.* Howard W. Sams, Indianapolis, 1978

Woolvet, G. A. *Transducers in Digital Systems.* Peter Peregrinus, Hitchin, Herts.,
1979

(4) Testing and Fault-finding

Bennetts, R. G. *Introduction to Digital Board Testing.* Edward Arnold, London,
1982

Coffron, J. W. *Practical Troubleshooting Techniques for Microprocessor Systems.* Prentice-Hall International, Hemel Hempstead, 1981

Coffron, J. W. *Using and Troubleshooting the Z8000.* Prentice-Hall International, Hemel Hempstead, 1982

Ghani, N. and Farrell, E. *Microprocessor System Debugging.* John Wiley,
Chichester, 1980

Kneen, J. *Logic Analyzers for Microprocessors.* John Wiley, Chichester, 1981

Lenk, J. D. *Handbook of Practical Microcomputer Troubleshooting.* Reston
Publishing Co., Reston, Virginia, 1979

Appendix A Pin Connections of the 8080 Family

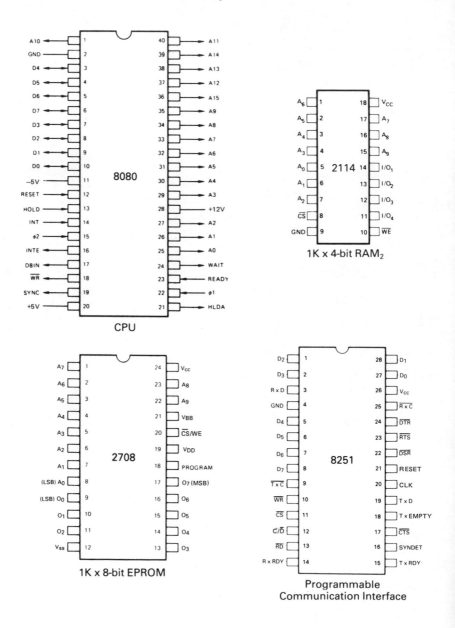

CPU

1K x 4-bit RAM₂

1K x 8-bit EPROM

Programmable
Communication Interface

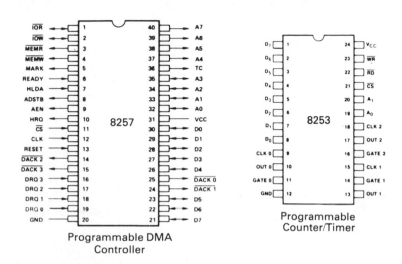

Programmable DMA
Controller

Programmable
Counter/Timer

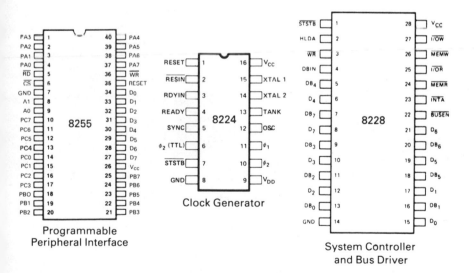

Programmable
Peripheral Interface

Clock Generator

System Controller
and Bus Driver

Appendix B Pin Connections of the 8085 Family

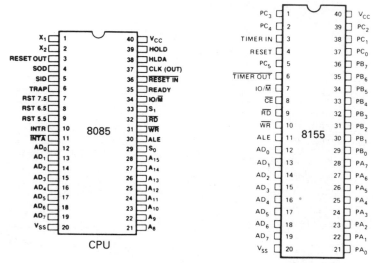

8085

Pin	Signal		Pin	Signal
1	X_1		40	V_{CC}
2	X_2		39	HOLD
3	RESET OUT		38	HLDA
4	SOD		37	CLK (OUT)
5	SID		36	RESET IN
6	TRAP		35	READY
7	RST 7.5		34	$IO/\overline{M}$
8	RST 6.5		33	S_1
9	RST 5.5		32	$\overline{RD}$
10	INTR		31	$\overline{WR}$
11	$\overline{INTA}$		30	ALE
12	AD_0		29	S_0
13	AD_1		28	A_{15}
14	AD_2		27	A_{14}
15	AD_3		26	A_{13}
16	AD_4		25	A_{12}
17	AD_5		24	A_{11}
18	AD_6		23	A_{10}
19	AD_7		22	A_9
20	V_{SS}		21	A_8

CPU

8155

Pin	Signal		Pin	Signal
1	PC_3		40	V_{CC}
2	PC_4		39	PC_2
3	TIMER IN		38	PC_1
4	RESET		37	PC_0
5	PC_5		36	PB_7
6	$\overline{TIMER\ OUT}$		35	PB_6
7	$IO/\overline{M}$		34	PB_5
8	$\overline{CE}$		33	PB_4
9	$\overline{RD}$		32	PB_3
10	$\overline{WR}$		31	PB_2
11	ALE		30	PB_1
12	AD_0		29	PB_0
13	AD_1		28	PA_7
14	AD_2		27	PA_6
15	AD_3		26	PA_5
16	AD_4		25	PA_4
17	AD_5		24	PA_3
18	AD_6		23	PA_2
19	AD_7		22	PA_1
20	V_{SS}		21	PA_0

256 byte Static RAM with I/O Ports and Timer

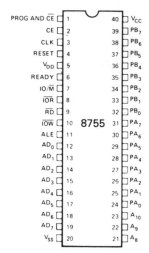

8755

Pin	Signal		Pin	Signal
1	PROG AND $\overline{CE}$		40	V_{CC}
2	CE		39	PB_7
3	CLK		38	PB_6
4	RESET		37	PB_5
5	V_{DD}		36	PB_4
6	READY		35	PB_3
7	$IO/\overline{M}$		34	PB_2
8	$\overline{IOR}$		33	PB_1
9	$\overline{RD}$		32	PB_0
10	$\overline{IOW}$		31	PA_7
11	ALE		30	PA_6
12	AD_0		29	PA_5
13	AD_1		28	PA_4
14	AD_2		27	PA_3
15	AD_3		26	PA_2
16	AD_4		25	PA_1
17	AD_5		24	PA_0
18	AD_6		23	A_{10}
19	AD_7		22	A_9
20	V_{SS}		21	A_8

2 K byte EPROM with I/O Ports

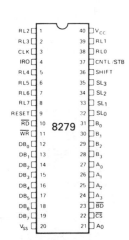

Programmable
Keyboard/Display Interface

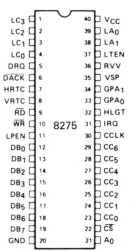

Programmable
CRT Controller

2K byte EPROM

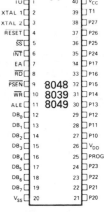

Single-chip
Microprocessor

Appendix C Pin Connections of the 6800 Family

1	V_{SS}	$\overline{Reset}$	40
2	$\overline{Halt}$	TSC	39
3	$\phi1$	N.C.	38
4	$\overline{IRQ}$	$\phi2$	37
5	VMA	DBE	36
6	$\overline{NMI}$	N.C.	35
7	BA	R/W	34
8	V_{CC}	D0	33
9	A0	D1	32
10	A1	D2	31
11	A2 **6800**	D3	30
12	A3	D4	29
13	A4	D5	28
14	A5	D6	27
15	A6	D7	26
16	A7	A15	25
17	A8	A14	24
18	A9	A13	23
19	A10	A12	22
20	A11	V_{SS}	21

CPU

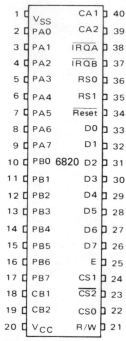

1	V_{SS}	CA1	40
2	PA0	CA2	39
3	PA1	$\overline{IRQA}$	38
4	PA2	$\overline{IRQB}$	37
5	PA3	RS0	36
6	PA4	RS1	35
7	PA5	$\overline{Reset}$	34
8	PA6	D0	33
9	PA7	D1	32
10	PB0 **6820**	D2	31
11	PB1	D3	30
12	PB2	D4	29
13	PB3	D5	28
14	PB4	D6	27
15	PB5	D7	26
16	PB6	E	25
17	PB7	CS1	24
18	CB1	$\overline{CS2}$	23
19	CB2	CS0	22
20	V_{CC}	R/W	21

Programmable Interface

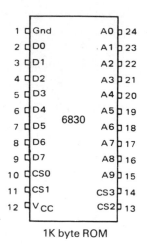

1	Gnd	A0	24
2	D0	A1	23
3	D1	A2	22
4	D2	A3	21
5	D3	A4	20
6	D4	A5	19
7	D5 **6830**	A6	18
8	D6	A7	17
9	D7	A8	16
10	CS0	A9	15
11	CS1	CS3	14
12	V_{CC}	CS2	13

1K byte ROM

1	V_{SS}	$\overline{CTS}$	24
2	Rx Data	$\overline{DCD}$	23
3	Rx Clk	D0	22
4	Tx Clk	D1	21
5	$\overline{RTS}$	D2	20
6	Tx Data	D3	19
7	$\overline{IRQ}$ **6850**	D4	18
8	CS0	D5	17
9	$\overline{CS2}$	D6	16
10	CS1	D7	15
11	RS	E	14
12	V_{DD}	R/W	13

Asynchronous Communication
Interface Adapter

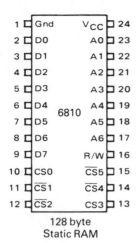

1	Gnd	V$_{CC}$	24
2	D0	A0	23
3	D1	A1	22
4	D2	A2	21
5	D3	A3	20
6	D4	A4	19
7	D5	A5	18
8	D6	A6	17
9	D7	R/W	16
10	CS0	$\overline{CS5}$	15
11	$\overline{CS1}$	$\overline{CS4}$	14
12	$\overline{CS2}$	CS3	13

6810

128 byte
Static RAM

1	V$_{SS}$	$\overline{C1}$	28
2	$\overline{G2}$	O1	27
3	O2	$\overline{G1}$	26
4	$\overline{C2}$	D0	25
5	$\overline{G3}$	D1	24
6	O3	D2	23
7	$\overline{C3}$	D3	22
8	Reset	D4	21
9	$\overline{IRQ}$	D5	20
10	RS0	D6	19
11	RS1	D7	18
12	RS2	Enable	17
13	R/$\overline{W}$	CS1	16
14	V$_{CC}$	$\overline{CS0}$	15

6840

Programmable
Timer Module

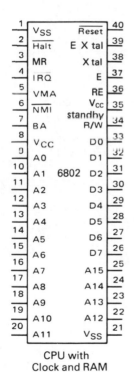

1	V$_{SS}$	Reset	40
2	$\overline{Halt}$	E X tal	39
3	MR	X tal	38
4	$\overline{IRQ}$	E	37
5	VMA	RE	36
6	$\overline{NMI}$	V$_{CC}$ standby	35
7	BA	R/W	34
8	V$_{CC}$	D0	33
9	A0	D1	32
10	A1	D2	31
11	A2	D3	30
12	A3	D4	29
13	A4	D5	28
14	A5	D6	27
15	A6	D7	26
16	A7	A15	25
17	A8	A14	24
18	A9	A13	23
19	A10	A12	22
20	A11	V$_{SS}$	21

6802

CPU with
Clock and RAM

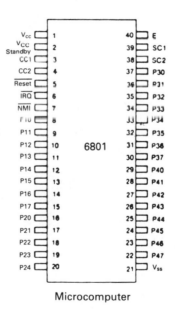

V$_{cc}$	1	40	E
V$_{CC}$ Standby	2	39	SC1
CC1	3	38	SC2
CC2	4	37	P30
Reset	5	36	P31
$\overline{IRQ}$	6	35	P32
$\overline{NMI}$	7	34	P33
P10	8	33	P34
P11	9	32	P35
P12	10	31	P36
P13	11	30	P37
P14	12	29	P40
P15	13	28	P41
P16	14	27	P42
P17	15	26	P43
P20	16	25	P44
P21	17	24	P45
P22	18	23	P46
P23	19	22	P47
P24	20	21	V$_{ss}$

6801

Microcomputer

Appendix D Pin Connections of the Z80 Family

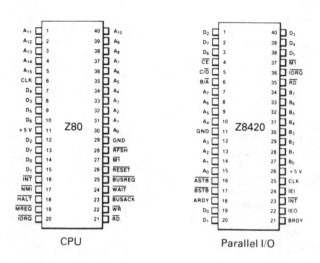

CPU

Parallel I/O

Serial I/O

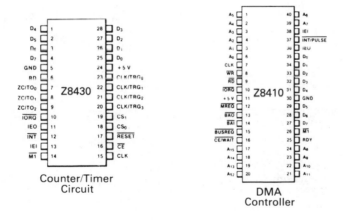

Counter/Timer
Circuit

DMA
Controller

Index